HISTORY OF THE WORLD

The Birth of Modern Europe

RSVP

RAINTREE
STECK-VAUGHN
PUBLISHERS
The Steck-Vaughn Company

Austin, Texas

This book has been reviewed for accuracy by
Bruce Taylor, PhD., University of Dayton

Passaggio al Mondo Moderno ©1990 by Editoriale Jaca Book, Milan

English translation copyright ©1993 by Steck-Vaughn Company

Italian text by Monica Dambrosio and Roberto Barbieri
Illustrations by Remo Berselli
English translation by Mary Di Ianni

Cover Illustration by Remo Berselli

Raintree Steck-Vaughn Editorial
Helene Resky: Editor

Raintree Steck-Vaughn Art/Production
D Childress: Art Director
Cynthia Ellis: Production Manager

Electronic Production
Management by Design

Printed and bound in the United States of America

1 2 3 4 5 6 7 8 9 0 WO 98 97 96 95 94 93

Library of Congress Cataloging-in-Publication Data
Dambrosio, Monica
    (Passaggio al Mondo Moderno. English)
    The Birth of Modern Europe / Italian text by Monica Dambrosio and Roberto Barbieri; illustrations by Remo Berselli; English translation by Mary Di Ianni).
        p.   cm. — (History of the world)
        Includes index.
        Summary: Surveys the history of Europe from the early 1300s through the mid-1500s, covering political, economic, and cultural changes that took place during that period.
        ISBN 0-8114-3325-0
        1. Europe –History – 476–1492 – Juvenile literature. (1. Europe –History – 476–1492. 2. Europe –History –1492–1648.) I. Barbieri, Roberto. II. Berselli, Remo, ill. III. Title. IV. Series.
D117.D36 1993
940.1 – dc20   92-22076
                                                                CIP
                                                                 AC

TABLE OF CONTENTS

THE SETTING

Europe in the Mid-Fifteenth Century

This map shows how Europe was divided politically in 1560, the end of the historical period covered in this book. From the early 1300s to the mid-1500s, Europe underwent profound economic, political, and cultural changes. Many modern European countries went through their formative stages during these 200 years.

The development of Europe's cities and states at this time fueled changes in other areas of life. Trade expanded as Europeans sought new routes to India and China, leading eventually to the exploration and settlement of the Americas.

Religious reform in Europe sparked conflicts between Protestants and Catholics. A cultural rebirth beginning in Italy led to new forms of literature, art, and music.

European political life between the fourteenth and sixteenth centuries was marked by several important factors. For hundreds of years, during a period of time called the *Reconquista*, the Spanish and the Portuguese had fought to reconquer the Iberian Peninsula from Muslim control. As this was achieved, Spain and Portugal grew stronger as nations, and the Spanish and the Portuguese turned their attention to exploration and trade. Eventually, both nations became major colonial powers.

In the meantime, France turned its attention toward Italy, which was a rich land, but politically weak and fragmented. In England, the Tudor family gained control of the country and started to develop it into a major power.

In Germany, the story was more complex. At this time, Germany was part of the Holy Roman Empire. Emperor Charles V wanted to make Germany the center of the Christian world, but the Protestant Reformation split Christianity, and the emperor's wish was never achieved. The Reformation further fragmented and divided a country already splintered by political differences.

The glorious cultural flowering of humanism and the Renaissance together with the economic vitality of the Italian cities not only failed to prevent, but, instead, advanced the political disintegration of the Italian peninsula. Economically and culturally rich, Italy became an object of conquest for other European powers.

Eastern Europe also had its share of change during this period. By conquering Hungary, the Ottoman Turks now shared borders with lands controlled by the Holy Roman Empire. Farther to the north, a new Russian nation emerged under the leadership of the Principality of Moscow.

Kingdom of Ireland

Kingdom of England

Bordeaux

Kingdom of Portugal

Lisbon

Madrid

Saragossa

Barcelona

Kingdom of Spain

Seville

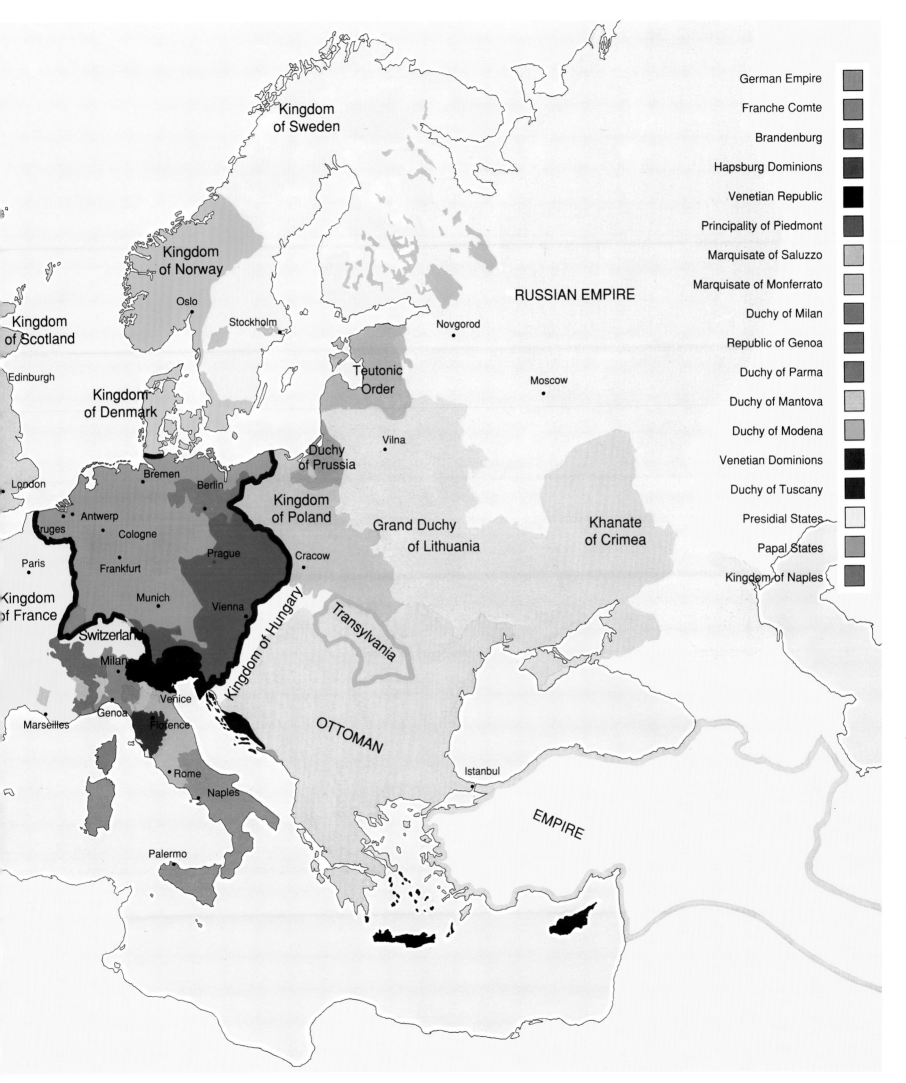

German Empire
Franche Comte
Brandenburg
Hapsburg Dominions
Venetian Republic
Principality of Piedmont
Marquisate of Saluzzo
Marquisate of Monferrato
Duchy of Milan
Republic of Genoa
Duchy of Parma
Duchy of Mantova
Duchy of Modena
Venetian Dominions
Duchy of Tuscany
Presidial States
Papal States
Kingdom of Naples

Kingdom
of Sweden

Kingdom
of Norway

Oslo

Kingdom
of Scotland

Edinburgh

Kingdom of Denmark

RUSSIAN EMPIRE

Stockholm

Novgorod

Teutonic
Order

Moscow

London

Bremen

Berlin

Duchy
of Prussia

Vilna

Antwerp

Bruges

Cologne

Kingdom
of Poland

Grand Duchy
of Lithuania

Khanate
of Crimea

Paris

Frankfurt

Prague

Cracow

Kingdom
of France

Munich

Vienna

Switzerland

Milan

Kingdom of Hungary

Transylvania

Genoa

Venice

OTTOMAN

Marseilles

Florence

Rome

Istanbul

Naples

EMPIRE

Palermo

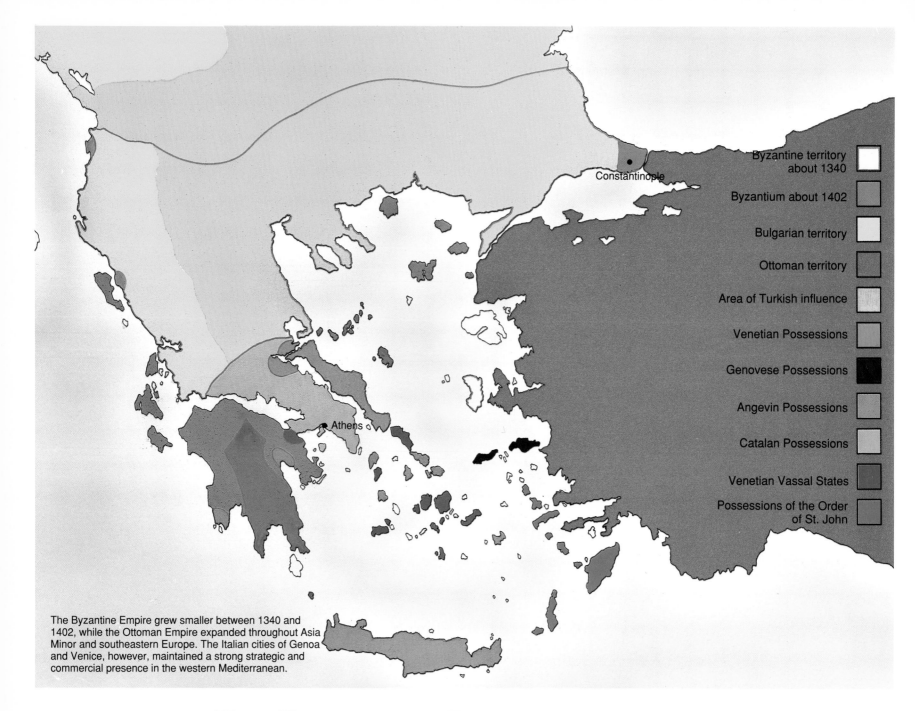

The Byzantine Empire grew smaller between 1340 and 1402, while the Ottoman Empire expanded throughout Asia Minor and southeastern Europe. The Italian cities of Genoa and Venice, however, maintained a strong strategic and commercial presence in the western Mediterranean.

Byzantine territory about 1340	
Byzantium about 1402	
Bulgarian territory	
Ottoman territory	
Area of Turkish influence	
Venetian Possessions	
Genovese Possessions	
Angevin Possessions	
Catalan Possessions	
Venetian Vassal States	
Possessions of the Order of St. John	

THE END OF THE BYZANTINE EMPIRE

The Byzantine Empire had once been the eastern half of the Roman Empire. After the collapse of Rome in A.D. 476, the eastern part of the empire survived. The capital was Constantinople, a great city built by the emperor Constantine on the site of the ancient Greek city of Byzantium. As time passed, the eastern empire became known as Byzantium, or the Byzantine Empire.

At its height, around A.D. 500, Byzantium ruled most of southeastern Europe, Asia Minor, some areas along the northern coast of Africa, and even parts of southern Italy. However, by the early part of the fourteenth century, Byzantium ruled only a small part of southeastern Europe, and the northwestern corner of what is now Turkey. Later, Byzantium lost most of its territory to the Ottoman Turks, who had their origins in Central Asia.

In 1204 Western European crusaders with Venetian economic support conquered Constantinople. The western leaders divided what was left of the Byzantine Empire among themselves and set up a new "Latin" Empire at Constantinople. This Latin Empire lasted until 1261 when a Greek general, Michael Palaeologus, defeated the western rulers of Constantinople and restored the Byzantine Empire.

The last two centuries of Byzantium, from 1261 to 1453, can be divided into two periods. The first period stretches from the time of re-establishment of the empire in 1261 to 1354, when the Ottoman Turks gained large areas of the Balkan Peninsula. The second period deals with the last hundred years of the empire, which finally collapsed completely when the Ottomans conquered Constantinople in 1453.

Michael Palaeologus ruled the restored Byzantium as Michael VIII. In order to consolidate his power and to expand it, Michael needed help from Western Europe. He turned to the strong Italian city of Genoa for aid and promised the Genoese trading rights in the lands he planned to conquer. Michael also sought help from the Roman Catholic church.

In 1054 Byzantine Christians had broken away from the control of Rome, but Michael planned to heal this split in Christianity. In 1274 he concluded an agreement with Pope Gregory X for the reunification of the two churches under the authority of Rome. In

reaching this agreement, Michael believed he had removed the most important stumbling block to good relations between Byzantium and the Catholic countries of Western Europe. He thought that Constantinople, as part of a unified Christian world, would have the Western Europeans as allies against the common enemy—the Muslim Turks.

Michael's plan did not work, however. The agreement with the pope came under attack by Orthodox church leaders in Byzantium, nor was it popular with the population. In Western Europe, support for the agreement collapsed when Pope Gregory X died.

Ninety Years of Slow Decline

Michael VIII was the last great Byzantine emperor. When he died in 1282, the empire was poised for disaster. The southern part of Greece, including Athens, was in western hands. Venice and Genoa possessed many

coastal areas and islands in former Byzantine lands and controlled trade. Meanwhile, the Serbs and Bulgarians were taking control of their lands in Albania, Epirus, Thessaly, and Macedonia away from the empire.

By far, though, the greatest threat to Byzantium came from the Ottoman Turks. During the next hundred years, the Ottomans expanded into southeastern Europe and conquered most of the lands around Constantinople. Gallipoli in 1354, Adrianopol in 1365, and then the lands of the Serbs and Bulgarians came under Ottoman control. Only Constantinople remained in Byzantine hands.

The Byzantine emperors traveled to Western Europe looking for help, but found none. As the Ottomans spread into Europe, the European leaders were more concerned about the threat to Hungary than they were about the fate of Constantinople. An army of Hungarians, Poles, and Romanians was formed to

As the Ottoman Turks came closer to capturing Constantinople, many of the city's residents tried to flee. But the exodus failed, and many people were killed when the Turks finally took the city.

defend Hungary, but the Turks defeated this army at the Battle of Varna in 1444.

After the defeat at Varna, the countries of Western Europe considered the complete collapse of the Byzantine Empire to be only a matter of time. Contacts between Europe and Constantinople became rarer, as Constantine XI, the last Byzantine emperor, tried in vain to get help from the west.

In the spring of 1453, Constantinople was surrounded and besieged by the Ottoman Turks. The city resisted, but was finally taken in late May. The sack of Constantinople lasted three days, and few of its inhabitants escaped. Finally, the Ottoman ruler, Muhammad II, entered the church of Santa Sophia in the city. The Byzantine Empire, the last remnant of the ancient Roman Empire, ceased to exist.

THE MONGOLS AND THE TURKS

Tamerlane

The Mongols were a nomadic people who, near the end of the eleventh century, had swept out of the plains of Central Asia, conquering everything in their path. Great Mongol leaders such as Genghis Khan, Batu Khan, and Kublai Khan created empires that stretched from China to Europe. Throughout much of the fourteenth century and into the early years of the fifteenth century, one of the most terrifying Mongol leaders was Timur the Lame, or Tamerlane.

Born around 1336 near Samarkand in Central Asia, Tamerlane's ambition was to restore the empire of Genghis Khan. In twenty-four years Tamerlane conquered much of Central Asia, Iran, Mesopotamia, Armenia, the Caucasus, and the eastern part of Anatolia. He also ruled over northern India and much of present-day Russia. Up to his sudden death in 1405, he dreamed of conquering China.

Wherever Tamerlane's Mongol forces went, they left results of their cruelty behind. Tamerlane destroyed much of the agriculture of Iran and Afghanistan when he conquered those territories. In Sivas, which is now part of Turkey, Tamerlane ordered four thousand Christians to be buried alive.

The Mongols believed in Islam, but Tamerlane's ferocity against other Muslims made them fear him greatly. After defeating the Ottoman Turks at Ankara in 1402, Tamerlane imprisoned and tortured the Turkish sultan and his sons. Though his conquests were impressive, Tamerlane had no precise ideas about how to govern. His empire fell apart rapidly after his death.

The Rise of Moscow

When the Mongols under Batu Khan swept over Russia in 1240, these conquerers came to be known as the Golden Horde. Under Mongol rule, Russia was divided into many principalities.

Some of these principalities had more power over local affairs than others. The Principality of Moscow enjoyed important administrative and political advantages under the Mongols, and this helped Moscow grow in power.

Arguments over who should rule the Golden Horde weakened it. Some of the Russian princes took advantage of this weakness to avoid paying taxes. The Horde temporarily reasserted its power, and in 1382, allied with Tamerlane, the Horde crushed a rebellion of the Russian princes.

This winged warrior is an example of Seljuk art. The Seljuks were a nomadic people from the plains of Central Asia. They were the first Turkish people to arrive in Byzantine territory.

This scene shows Muhammad II meeting with his counselors. The meeting takes place outside a tent hung with splendid carpets. Although the Ottomans ruled a mighty empire, the tents show that they had not forgotten their nomadic past. On the other hand, the rich carpets reveal the Ottoman taste for refinement.

During the next hundred years, however, the Principality of Moscow grew stronger, and in 1480, under the leadership of Ivan III, Moscow refused to pay any more taxes to the Golden Horde. By this time the Horde had shrunk in size and power, and was too weak to control Ivan. The rulers of Moscow had become the most powerful leaders in Russia.

The Ottoman Empire

The Ottomans were a Turkish tribe from the steppes of Central Asia that had moved into Byzantine Anatolia. The Ottomans were fierce warriors, and they fought under the Seljuk dynasty. The Seljuks were the first Turkish people to establish their rule in Anatolia.

The first Ottoman dynasty was established under Osman (1290–1326) who spread Ottoman control throughout Anatolia. Under Murad I, Turkish power expanded toward the Balkans, the Black Sea, and the Adriatic Sea.

In 1402 Tamerlane temporarily stopped the Turkish spread of power. After Tamerlane's death, the Ottomans reasserted their strength with amazing speed. They firmly established their empire in eastern Europe by decisively beating the Europeans at the Battle of Varna in 1444. For eight hundred years the Islamic world had dreamed of conquering Constantinople, and in 1453 Muhammad II achieved that dream.

In his new capital, which is known as present-day Istanbul, Muhammad II concentrated on the task of organizing a government for his empire. He published the first Turkish legal code. He did not force non-Muslims to convert to Islam. He also granted important commercial privileges to the Christians living in the conquered lands.

Muhammad II had the foresight to appoint Scolarios as patriarch (religious leader) of Constantinople. Scolarios had strongly opposed any unification with the Roman Catholic church. By appointing Scolarios as patriarch, Muhammad II created an effective obstacle against any further western influence among the Eastern Orthodox population. The office of patriarch was the only imperial Byzantine institution to survive, and this gave the people living in former Byzantine areas a chance to keep their own cultural identity.

The years after 1453 became an era of Ottoman cultural rebirth. The Turks, eager to learn more about different civilizations, studied the cultures of Iran, India, China, and Europe. In this way, the Turks welcomed a wide variety of artistic influences. Thus, the Ottomans of the fifteenth century retained the traditional desire of the peoples of the Central Asian steppes to learn about distant cultures.

Tamerlane's mausoleum, which was built in Samarkand between 1490 and 1501, is a magnificent example of the Central Asian style of architecture common at the time.

THE HUNDRED YEARS WAR: FROM 1337 TO THE END OF THE FOURTEENTH CENTURY

Origins of the War

From 1337 to 1453, France and England fought a series of wars that are known collectively as the Hundred Years War. These wars were fought mostly in France and caused great devastation. As with all wars, the Hundred Years War was fought for many reasons—economic, political, and social. But another cause of the Hundred Years War was the intermarriage among the ruling families of both France and England.

In 1314 King Philip IV (Philip the Fair) of France died. Philip belonged to the ruling Capetian family in France, which was founded by Hugh Capet in A.D. 987. At the time of Philip's death, the Capetian monarchy was the most powerful in Europe. A large number of royal officials with legal training managed the kingdom for the sovereign. These officials enforced justice and collected taxes, performing jobs that had once been done by the nobles. Philip's daughter, Isabella, married the English king, Edward II. Their son, Edward III, would later claim the French throne because his mother was a Capet.

Although the Capetians had established a certain stability in France, the monarchy underwent periods of deep unrest. The king's authority was weak in Brittany and in other areas, especially in Flanders, where the people did not speak French. The cities of Ghent and Bruges in Flanders particularly defied French rule. The situation was made worse in 1328 when the last Capetian king, Charles IV, died leaving no male heirs.

Charles was succeeded by his cousin, Philip VI of the Valois family, but this succession was challenged by King Edward III of England who, because his mother was a Capetian, claimed that he should inherit the French crown.

In fact, the kingdoms of France and England were linked by a series of complex intermarriages and territorial exchanges dating back to the tenth century. The Plantagenet family that ruled England spoke French and followed many of the same customs as the Capetians of France. To make matters more complicated, the English kings ruled Gascony in France and were therefore, supposedly, subjects of the king of France.

The English presence on French soil had been the object of endless conflicts between France and England for centuries, and was one of the immediate causes of the Hundred Years War. Edward III wanted to expand his holdings in Gascony. He formed alliances with the Flemish cities, crossed the English Channel, and in 1340 had himself crowned king of France.

Edward defeated the French at the Battle of Crécy in 1346, and went on to capture the French port city of Calais. The English were very successful in exploiting France's internal struggles against the French monarchy. After Philip VI died, a rebellion broke out in Normandy against his successor, John II. The English defeated John's forces at Poitiers, captured the king, and held him in England for ransom.

The splendid court of the Valois kings had little in common with the frugal, somber court of the Capetians. The quest for eccentricity reached its peak during the reign of Charles VI, when banquets and celebrations were held in an almost fairy-tale atmosphere.

New fashions of all kinds became increasingly popular. Hennins, tall cone-shaped headdresses, were so popular that Queen Isabel had all the doors in the castle at Vincennes made high enough to give the ladies sufficient headroom when wearing their hennins.

This illustration shows one of the celebrations held at the court of Charles VI. The king and several of his nobles disguised themselves as wild men and covered their faces and bodies with feathers. The costumes caught fire, and several people were burned to death. Charles was saved by the duchess of Berry who put out the flames of his burning costume by covering him with her cape. This incident is sometimes known as the "Feast of the Burning Dancers."

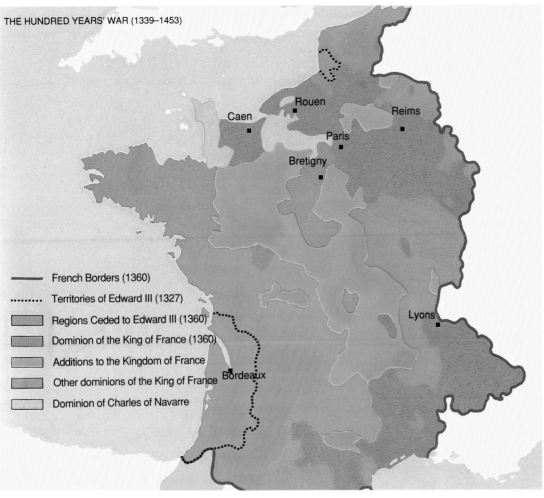

THE HUNDRED YEARS' WAR (1339–1453)

Caen · Rouen · Reims
Paris ·
Bretigny ·
Lyons ·
Bordeaux

— French Borders (1360)
········· Territories of Edward III (1327)
▢ Regions Ceded to Edward III (1360)
▢ Dominion of the King of France (1360)
▢ Additions to the Kingdom of France
▢ Other dominions of the King of France
▢ Dominion of Charles of Navarre

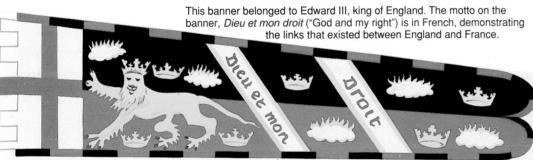

This banner belonged to Edward III, king of England. The motto on the banner, *Dieu et mon droit* ("God and my right") is in French, demonstrating the links that existed between England and France.

This object belonged to Charles VI. When Charles went insane, his incapacity to govern created unrest among the French nobles. Working with Queen Isabel, Louis of Orléans, and Philip the Bold, the duke of Burgundy tried to rule the country.

Divisions Among the French Nobility

The kingdom was now under the control of John's son, Charles (later to be Charles V), who had to deal with unrest among the French nobles and revolts throughout France, as well as fight the English. Finally, a truce was negotiated with the English at Bretigny in 1360. Under the terms of the truce, King John II returned to France, and Edward accepted expanded borders in Gascony but gave up his claim to be king of France.

After John II died, Charles V reorganized the French kingdom and regained Navarre and Burgundy, some of the territory that had been lost. He made his brother, Philip, duke of Burgundy, thus insuring support from that part of country. When war flared up again in 1369, Charles took back some of the lands that had been lost around Gascony.

Charles V died in 1380, and he was succeeded by his son Charles VI, who was only eleven years old. Because the king was so young, the great nobles in France vied with each other to control him. Philip the Bold, duke of Burgundy, John of Berry, and Louis of Anjou were more than eager to manage the kingdom. Charles V's counselors, nicknamed *Marmousets* (little fellows), tried to keep these nobles in check.

Charles ruled for 42 years. This was a time of pomp and ostentation at the royal court. Sumptuous banquets were held in an almost fairy-tale atmosphere. As the years passed, the climate at court began to sour as the king suffered from periods of insanity. The differences between the powerful nobles and the *Marmousets* became increasingly violent. Finally, the kingdom was taken over by the queen, Isabel of Bavaria, the king's brother, Louis of Orléans, and Philip of Burgundy.

A division within the French nobility now took place. The rivalry between the duke of Orléans and the duke of Burgundy grew intense. Philip the Bold died and was succeeded by John the Fearless. When the duke of Orléans was assassinated, the French nobility split into two camps, and conflict between the two groups erupted into full-scale civil war. This division within the French nobility was the direct cause of another English invasion of northwestern France.

This effigy of Edward III was sculpted on his tomb ten years after his death. Edward's mother was the daughter of King Philip IV of France. Therefore, Edward III felt he had a claim to the French throne, and he gave up this claim only when he gained more territory in southeastern France.

THE HUNDRED YEARS WAR: FROM 1415 TO ITS CONCLUSION IN 1453

France Divided and Invaded

In 1415, the English again invaded France. Under the leadership of Henry V, the English captured Harfleur and defeated the French at the Battle of Agincourt. In 1417 Henry invaded France again. The war went badly for the French as the English took the city of Rouen and extended their control over all of Normandy.

Royal power in France was divided in two parts. On one side, King Charles VI and the queen were under the influence of the duke of Burgundy; on the other side was the dauphin (the title given to the king's eldest son), the future Charles VII, who established his court at Bourges.

The alliance between the duke of Burgundy and England forced Charles VI to sign the Treaty of Troyes in 1420. Under this treaty, Henry V, the king of England, was recognized as the heir to the French throne. Ironically, both Charles V and Henry V died in the same year. In effect, France was divided into three parts. The English controlled Normandy and most of northern France; the duke of Burgundy controlled northeastern France, and the dauphin controlled the south.

Joan of Arc: the Revolt and the Tragedy

The story of Joan of Arc's military activities is quite brief. She was born in 1412 in the village of Domrémy and began her military career at seventeen. Because of her devotion and strength of conviction, the dauphin put her in command of his army. In 1429 she broke the English siege of Orléans and defeated them at Patay.

She then accompanied the dauphin to Reims where he was crowned Charles VII, king of France. Her aim was to free Paris, but she failed. She was captured by forces loyal to the duke of Burgundy and turned over to the English. Condemned as a heretic, she was burned at the stake in Rouen in 1431.

Although her military career was short, she was able to channel the common people's discontent with the war into action. This discontent in the lands occupied by the English was very strong and often caused peasant revolts. Joan was able to give these rebellions a strong focus.

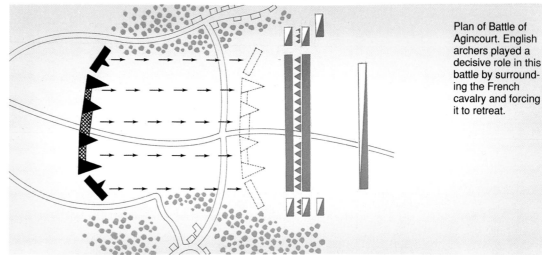

Plan of Battle of Agincourt. English archers played a decisive role in this battle by surrounding the French cavalry and forcing it to retreat.

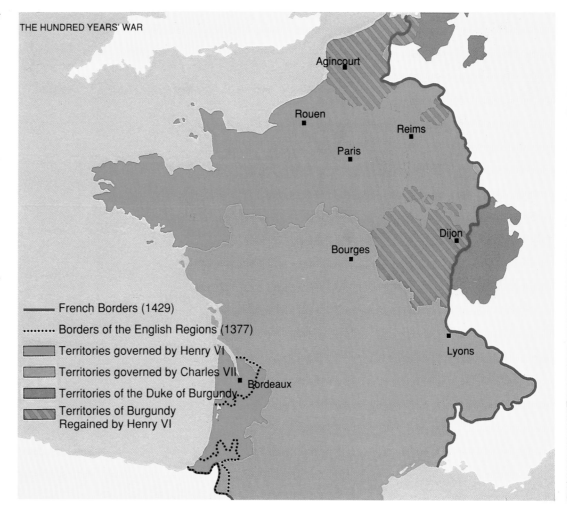

THE HUNDRED YEARS' WAR

——— French Borders (1429)

········ Borders of the English Regions (1377)

Territories governed by Henry VI

Territories governed by Charles VII

Territories of the Duke of Burgundy

Territories of Burgundy Regained by Henry VI

This is the only existing contemporary portrait of Joan of Arc. Joan was able to channel the widespread discontent of the French people into direct action against the English. Her brief military career helped change the course of events in the Hundred Years War.

After Joan's death, the French court fell into disarray until the duke of Burgundy took the initiative that brought about a change. The duke and the new king, Charles VII, reached an agreement that gave more territory to the duke in exchange for his loyalty to the crown.

Troops loyal to Charles entered Paris in 1436, but it would take many more years before they would gain control of all the land around the capital. The French regained control of Normandy in 1450 and English power in Gascony was severely weakened. By 1453, the English controlled only Calais, which they held until 1558.

Changes Caused by the War

The Hundred Years War had caused deep social ills and widespread destruction. War had become an everyday reality for the French. One French writer wrote, "There are men who have never known what peace is, not even in the stories told by their ancestors."

Many changes in the way wars were fought took place during the Hundred Years War. The use of gunpowder was the biggest change. It resulted in the development of heavier armor for soldiers. This armor was very cumbersome and could weigh over one hundred pounds. Because of the armor's weight, fighting on horseback was very difficult. This type of armor was worn almost exclusively by nobles.

Another innovation of the Hundred Years War was the use of large numbers of mercenaries, hired soldiers who would fight for anyone who paid them. These adventurers formed roving bands and continued their raids even during times of truce. These bands scoured the countryside robbing and killing.

The war also changed the way taxes were levied. The conflict was very expensive, and the rulers decided each family group or "fireside" would have to be taxed to pay for it. When John II was captured, the English demanded a high ransom for his release. The ransom was so large that it could not be collected in one year. Therefore, a tax was collected every year, and it was kept in place long after John II died. The tax was one more reason why the Hundred Years War was a disastrous event for the French people and contributed to the economic crisis of the period.

Weapons using gunpowder were first used in the Hundred Years War. These weapons caused changes in the type of body armor worn. Heavier suits of armor were needed to protect the body from artillery blasts. If a noble wearing this armor fell off his horse, it was hard for him to get up again. He was either killed, or more likely, captured and held for ransom.

Europe's population in the fourteenth century was greatly reduced by outbreaks of the plague, recurring famines, and by almost constant warfare.

Many people who lived in the countryside moved to the cities where they thought they would be safer. As the population of the farms and countryside shrank, less land was cultivated, and the abandoned fields were reclaimed by woods or turned into pasture for cattle.

The highest death rates from the plague were not in the countryside but in the cities, especially among the poor who lived in unhealthy, overcrowded conditions. Doctors and government officials who, because of the nature of their work, stayed in the cities also fell easy victims of the plague.

The picture below shows peasants entering the Spanish city of León where they hoped to escape the plague.

EUROPE IN CRISIS

Famine and the Plague

One of the most violent and difficult periods in European history took place between 1340 and 1430. During this period, peasants and city-dwellers alike had to deal with violence, famine, and plague on almost a daily basis.

Great progress in agriculture and trade had been made in Europe between the eleventh and thirteenth centuries, resulting in long periods of relative prosperity. New farming methods had increased the quality and quantity of harvests. New villages had sprung up and cities had grown larger.

But farmlands had been cultivated almost exclusively with grains like wheat and barley. When these crops failed, food supplies decreased. After 1300, year after year of too much rain at the wrong time also reduced harvests, and passing bands of mercenaries and large armies all but destroyed the countryside. Normal farming was disrupted for long periods of time. The food supply fell, and the first famines occurred between 1309 and 1320, causing many deaths. They were followed by the first outbreaks of the bubonic plague in 1347.

In October 1347, several Genoese ships returning from the Crimea discharged their passengers in Messina, Sicily. Some of these passengers already had the bubonic plague. The plague spread rapidly, and after only a few weeks, almost all of Italy was stricken.

In December, a ship carrying passengers infected with the plague landed in Marseilles, France, and soon the plague was spreading throughout Europe. Between 1348 and 1349, the plague devastated France, the British Isles, Holland, Austria, Scandinavia, and Spain. After 1350, the plague reappeared from time to time for almost one hundred years.

The bubonic plague was a terrible thing to see. Victims were covered with blister-like pustules and suffered from swollen lymph glands and convulsions. The victims vomited blood and usually died after three days of terrible suffering. Corpses were contagious for at least 48 hours, and the measures taken to stop the plague were completely ineffective.

The failure of the medical profession to prevent or cure the plague led people to believe that the plague was the result of a diabolical spell. Lepers, beggars, and anyone unpopular with the crowd were accused of poisoning water supplies and spreading the diseases. Mobs committed massacre after massacre adding more death and destruction.

Although research has shown the plague was caused by fleas carrying the disease from infected animals to humans, the reasons for its rapid spread are still not clear. Death rates were higher in cities than the countryside, and overcrowded city dwellings contributed to the spread of the disease. The poor, crammed into tiny rooms without light or air, fell easy victims to the plague as did government officials, doctors, and others who worked in the cities.

At first, the plague seemed to hit mostly adults, but successive waves hit children hardest. Between the beginning of the fourteenth century and the middle of the fifteenth, about one-quarter of Europe's population was wiped out by the plague.

The Fall in the Population

The deadly combination of famine and plague halted the increase in Europe's population that had been growing steadily from the eleventh century. Poor harvests meant that many young people could not afford to marry until later in life. They also had fewer children.

But the effects of these disasters on future generations were not as devastating as might be expected. The price of grain fell because even though there were fewer farmers to cultivate the land, more grain was produced than the smaller population could use. Famine was now less of a threat, and farmers could turn to other needed crops such as flax used in making linen.

Raising animals, especially sheep, began to be more profitable than raising crops. Large landowners were able to keep huge, profitable flocks that did not need many people to look after them.

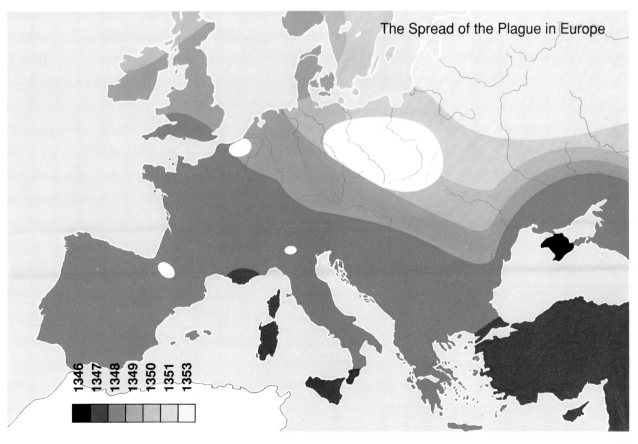

The Spread of the Plague in Europe

1346 1347 1348 1349 1350 1351 1353

REBELLIONS IN THE CITIES AND IN THE COUNTRYSIDE

Causes of the Rebellions

The combination of economic crisis, war, famine, and plague shook European society to its core in the fourteenth century. In the countryside, the nobles reacted to the drop in grain prices by growing other crops or raising livestock. Both activities displaced many peasants. The nobles seized land that the villagers previously had the right to use and forced the peasants to do more work.

Many peasants moved to the cities. But in the cities, the guilds refused to take in new members. Consequently, the number of unskilled workers rose, and they had difficulty finding employment. Their poverty contrasted greatly with the nobles' riches.

Both rural and urban populations had to pay taxes to support the government and pay for the wars the governments waged. Whereas poor people could once find comfort in the teachings of religion, even the church was beginning to lose some of its authority.

The Geography of the Revolts

In many ways, rebellions, like hunger, wars, and plague, became an almost daily occurrence in fourteenth century Europe. The unsatisfied needs of the people for food and security often motivated the rebellions. In 1358 France was shaken by two revolts, one in Paris and one in the countryside.

The revolt in Paris was led by Etienne Marcel who was a member of one of the richest families in Paris. Marcel organized a protest against the new taxes the French government had levied to finance the war against England. He was also the leader of merchants who felt they did not have enough influence with the government. In February 1358, a mob headed by Marcel broke into the palace and forced the dauphin to flee. Paris remained in rebel hands until July when Marcel was killed.

Paris was not the only city that felt the sting of rebellion. The same type of revolts took place in cities in Germany and Flanders.

Acts of sabotage and refusal to work were common in the cities. Between 1378 and 1383 there were a series of violent demonstrations among the working classes of many European cities. In Florence in 1378, the working classes attacked two government palaces. They did get some representation in the city government but were unable to reorganize city life. The major guilds of Florence asked the nobles for help. Order was restored at the end of 1381.

Rebellion was not confined to the cities during the fourteenth century. For fifteen days in 1358, France went through a series of revolts in the countryside. The revolts were led by the Jacques, a nickname given to French peasants. The peasants were tired of the long war and opposed to paying new taxes. The revolts were short and violent as bands of Jacques were defeated and destroyed in northern France.

In England, however, there was a strong, well-organized peasant revolt in 1381 in the county of Essex. The peasants revolted against the economic conditions under which they lived. The leader of this revolt was Wat Tyler who led the peasants on a march to Canterbury and then to London, burning public buildings in both places. The king met with Tyler and promised to support changes, but Tyler was captured and killed by the mayor of London's forces, and the revolt was crushed.

Along with revolts in the countryside, came increased attacks of bandits and thieves. Some peasants, suffering from overwork, lack of food, and heavy taxation became outlaws robbing merchants and travelers. However, they did not usually raid the houses of the nobles.

Revolts in Flanders and in the Holy Roman Empire

Some of the deepest unrest during this period was felt in the countryside of Flanders, where a bitter war devastated the region around the cities of Bruges and Ypres. After years of drought and severe winters, the peasants revolted when new taxes were levied on them. The rebellion was, for the most part, a peasant uprising that began with the peasants forming village assemblies and committing acts of violence against the nobles and government officials. The revolt spread quickly to the cities, Bruges in particular.

The revolt in Flanders is historically important because the rebels not only revolted against economic conditions, but also wanted to change the accepted Flemish social order. The rebels wanted to free themselves of control by the nobility, and they turned against anyone who represented the old order, including judges and tax collectors.

The uprising in Flanders, which lasted for five years, was well-organized and had good leaders. The rebels were decisive and courageous and were defeated only when the count of Flanders asked the French king for help. The king defeated the rebels at Cassel in 1328. As always, the defeat was followed by imprisonments and executions.

In 1379 another rebellion shook Flanders. The cause of this rebellion was probably a conflict between the cities of Bruges and Ghent over the building of a canal that would have cut Ghent off from certain lines of business. The boatmen of Ghent were the first to rise up, and they were followed immediately by weavers in Ghent. Soon the weavers of Bruges and Ypres joined in.

The count of Flanders' officials fled the area, and the rebels were in command for

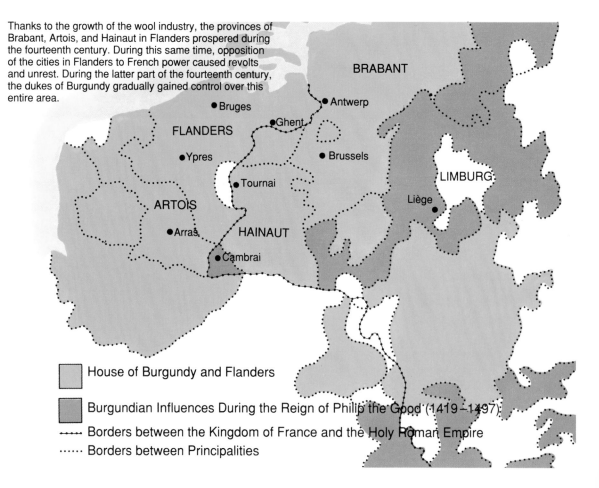

Thanks to the growth of the wool industry, the provinces of Brabant, Artois, and Hainaut in Flanders prospered during the fourteenth century. During this same time, opposition of the cities in Flanders to French power caused revolts and unrest. During the latter part of the fourteenth century, the dukes of Burgundy gradually gained control over this entire area.

BRABANT
• Bruges
• Antwerp
• Ghent
FLANDERS
• Ypres
• Brussels
• Tournai
LIMBURG
ARTOIS
• Liège
• Arras
HAINAUT
• Cambrai

☐ House of Burgundy and Flanders
☐ Burgundian Influences During the Reign of Philip the Good (1419–1497)
---- Borders between the Kingdom of France and the Holy Roman Empire
...... Borders between Principalities

The florin is a gold coin that was minted by the city of Florence. In the fourteenth century, the more powerful Italian cities minted their own money. Economic and political power in these cities became concentrated in the hands of a small number of people. Often, the family with the most economic power also gained political control over a city.

a time. The rebels tried to restore the old forms of local government, but conflicts among the rebels weakened the revolt. Philip van Artevelde, the leader of the rebellion, was able to keep the rebellion from disintegrating, and for a while he was the real governor of Flanders. Once again, the king of France stepped in and his army defeated the rebels at Roosebeke in 1382.

Germany also had its share of rebellions. A number of German cities, especially Lubeck, were troubled by uprisings. On the whole, these uprisings were protests against heavy taxation or attempts by different guilds to gain more local power.

Revolts, Unrest, and Change

Rebellions and revolts took place throughout most of the fourteenth century. Though the causes of these rebellions were not always the same, certain themes kept reappearing.

In the countryside, the peasants wanted to free themselves from the oppression of the nobles and the government officials. In the towns, the rebellions were a form of protests by all those excluded from power, especially the new middle class who wanted more power and prestige in local government.

The economic crisis, the plague, and the decrease in population shook European medieval society. The drop in prices for grain crops prompted landholders to raise different crops or turn their land into pastures with complete disregard for the peasant's traditional ways of life. Some peasants reacted by becoming outlaws and bandits, as shown in this picture.

The peasants, the workers, and the minor guilds that revolted were all defeated. The members of these groups would become the objects of long and violent repression. Their struggle to exist in a system of oligarchy, or rule by the few, and bureaucracy would be one of the characteristics of modern nations and states.

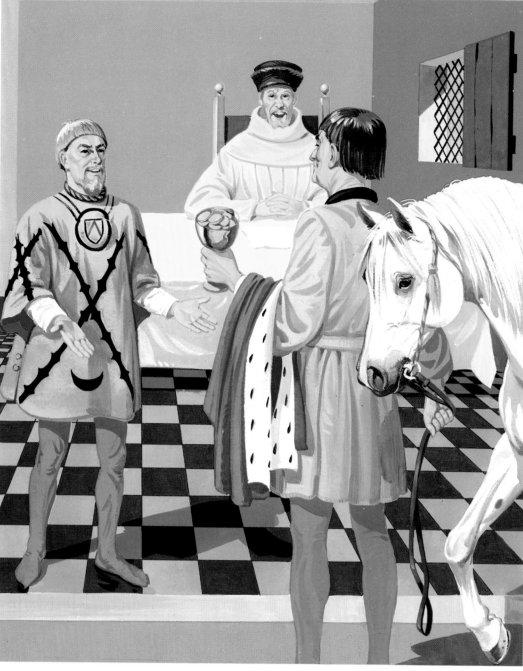

Above: The great Italian writer Giovanni Boccaccio was born in 1313 in Tuscany but lived many years in Naples. Boccaccio is considered one of the three most important Italian writers, along with Dante and Petrarch. He was the first great prose writer, and in his major work, *The Decameron*, he drew a shrewd portrait of Italian society during his time.
Below: An example of the work produced by Italian goldsmiths during the fourteenth century.

The above scene is based on documents in the Vatican Library and inspired by a short story, "Bergamini and the Great Cane della Scalla" which is in *The Decameron*. In the story, Boccaccio describes the generosity of the great Cane della Scalla, the lord of Verona. Bergamini, a shrewd speaker, tells the great della Scalla the tale of Primasso, a well-spoken man, just like Bergamini himself, who because of his story-telling abilities, receives precious gifts from a rich church official. At the end of Bergamini's story, the lord of Verona, eager to show his own generosity, gives Bergamini a magnificent horse, rich clothes, and gold coins.

POLITICAL CHANGES IN ITALY

The Seigniories

Between 1250 and 1350, cities in Italy experienced changes in how they were governed. Many of these cities had been *communi*, cities that governed themselves. But as one family, or one individual rose to dominate city life, the Italian cities became seigniories, cities or territories under the control of a seignior, or lord. In Milan the change was led by Ottone Visconti, who dominated the guilds. The Este family controlled Ferrara, Modena, and Reggio in the same way.

In general, the development of a seigniory was an outgrowth and extension of the work done by the most important leaders of the city when it was a commune. For example, in Verona, Mastino della Scala had held the position of *capitano del popolo*, literally, "Captain of the people." This title was given to a magistrate who was supposed to look after the interests of the people in the city for a period of one year. Mastino della Scala, however, passed the title on to his grandchildren, and they consolidated their hold on the position.

Changes like this did not cause the commune to disappear immediately. The transition usually took place gradually. The seignior slowly took on more political, military, diplomatic, and financial duties, and he chose a council of experts to help him govern the city. The citizens of a city gradually became the lord's subjects, and he tried to extend his control over the surrounding countryside. Eventually, his position became hereditary, passing from one generation to the next.

Not all the cities followed this pattern. The governing power in Venice was in the hands of

Soldiers of fortune were common in fourteenth century Italy. Mercenaries often got involved in politics, and several acquired control over cities or other territories.

Matteo Palmieri was a typical example of the intellectuals and scholars of fourteenth century Italy. These scholars, called Humanists, not only carried out literary and legal studies but also used their knowledge to serve their cities. Many held important political positions.

a small group of people, an oligarchy, rather than in the hands of a single family. On several occasions, certain nobles tried to take power, but each was defeated by the oligarchy.

In central Italy, the transition to single family rule was slower than in the north. Florence did not come under the control of the Medici family until 1434 when Cosimo de' Medici used people working for him to take control of the city. The rise of the Medici family is typical of Italian politics at the time. An important merchant became a public figure because he had many people indebted to him, and he supported relatives through whom he could control city life.

The rise of single family rule also took place in some of the cities in the Papal States. In 1305 the popes took up residence in the French city of Avignon, and Rome fell into disorder. The nobles in and around Rome fought each other for more power. In 1347 a man named Cola di Rienzo led a working-class

movement against the nobility and took control of the city. The pope excommunicated Rienzo, who left the city. With the help of the Holy Roman emperor, Rienzo returned to power in 1353, but within a year he was killed. After Rienzo's death, the pope tried to re-establish his authority throughout the Papal States, but was only partially successful.

Rule in Italy south of the Papal States was divided between the House of Avignon in France and the House of Aragon in Spain.

Sicily came under control of the Aragon dynasty in 1302. During the fourteenth century the power of the nobility in Sicily increased, until finally a small number of families ruled the island. In 1323 Sardinia was added to Aragon's possessions.

On the Italian mainland the kingdom of Naples was ruled by the Angevins, French nobles related to the Capetian kings of France. Under Robert of Angevin (1309–1343), the

kingdom enjoyed a period of political calm and cultural prosperity.

When the rule of the Angevins weakened in southern Italy, the pope, the French, and the Aragons all showed interest in the area. The pope, however, had been weakened by the move to Avignon, and the Papal States were not strong enough to extend their power.

France had problems, too. The Hundred Years War was still raging, and France was not as strong as it had once been. Aragon, which already governed Sicily and Sardinia, now could expand its power to the Italian mainland.

The attempt to extend Aragon rule began in 1421 and was opposed by the pope, the republic of Genoa, and the Angevins in Naples. Through the clever use of military power, gold, and diplomacy, Alfonso of Aragon was able to drag his enemies into endless years of war. Finally, strengthened by an alliance with Milan, Alfonso's army entered Naples in 1442.

ITALY IN THE FIFTEENTH CENTURY

The Growth of Milan and Venice

The Italian peninsula has always been of strategic, political, and geographic interest to the rest of Europe. During the first half of the fifteenth century, however, the major European powers at that time — France and the Holy Roman Empire — were mostly involved with their own internal problems and left Italy alone.

During this period, many of the major Italian political centers — Milan, Venice, Florence — increased their territories and grew into regional states. This transition was marked by internal political intrigue, wars, and intermarriages between ruling families. The result was a constant changing of the territorial boundaries in northern and central Italy.

Under the leadership of Gian Galeazzo Visconti, Milan added the cities of Verona, Bologna, Bergamo, Brescia, Perugia, and part of the territory of Padua to its domain between 1378 and 1402. Eventually, even the great merchant city of Genoa was conquered by Milan.

In the meantime, Venice was expanding both along the eastern coasts of the Adriatic and to the west. The Republic of Florence added Arezzo in 1384, Pisa in 1405, and Livorno in 1421.

The struggle between the major Italian states reached its peak in 1447 when Milan, after the death of Filippo Maria Visconti, declared itself a republic. Old and new enemies prepared to invade Milan, and the city called upon the great military leader Francesco Sforza to aid it. Sforza was accepted as the duke of Milan in 1450, and he negotiated a peace treaty with Venice at Lodi in 1454. All the other Italian states eventually agreed to abide by the Peace of Lodi.

The Balance of Power

In the second half of the fifteenth century, Italian society benefited from the leadership and guidance of Lorenzo de' Medici, often called Lorenzo the Magnificent. The Medici family ruled Florence, and under Lorenzo, it became one of the most powerful states in Italy. Lorenzo not only helped beautify Florence with many great works of art, he also used the city's power to maintain relative peace throughout Italy. This period was also marked by the influence of open-minded politicians and popes.

The apparent stability hid deep unrest. Many of the noble families living in the Italian states had special privileges that the princes were slow to abolish. Attempts to remove these privileges were often met with violence and rebellion on the part of the nobles.

Another weakness of the Italian states was their inability to organize an effective method of taxation. At a time when military expenses were high and the number of government officials rose, taxation was poorly regulated and never covered the growing expenses.

Throughout the fifteenth century, during one of the most important periods of cultural rebirth in Italy, internal peace and order was fragile. No single power was fully able to exploit the many resources of the Italian peninsula.

The fact that Italy was fragmented into many states made it easier for other European powers to reassert their interest in Italy. At the end of the fifteenth century, several European powers became involved in the quarrels between the Italian states. In 1493 Charles VII of France, as heir of the Angevins, claimed the crown of Naples. Charles formed an alliance with Milan, and went on to win the kingdom of Naples away from the Aragon family. This action precipitated a period of conflict known as the Italian Wars.

After Charles VIII died, the kingdom of Naples returned to Aragon rule. As the Italian Wars dragged on into the sixteenth century, the Peace of Lodi vanished, and the French, the Spanish, and the Germans all fought for control over parts of Italy.

Above: Portrait of Lorenzo the Magnificent
Left: Portrait of Girolamo Savonarola a reformer and Dominican Friar who drove Piero de' Medici from power in Florence with the aid of Charles VIII. Advocating an ideal state, Savonarola denied the pope's immortality among other things. In retaliation Pope Alexander VI declared the friar a heretic and had him excommunicated and finally hanged.

Map of fifteenth century Italy showing the numerous individual states in the Italian peninsula.

Map labels: Duchy of Savoy; Duchy of Milan; Venetian Republic; Este; Republic of Genoa; Republic of Florence; Republic of Siena; Papal States; Kingdom of Naples

This scene shows the courtyard of the Ca' Granda in Milan. Ca' Granda was originally a hospital for sick, poor people in Milan. It was founded by Francesco Sforza, duke of Milan, in 1456 and designed by Filarete. Today the Ca' Granda is the center of the Faculty of Humanities of the University of Milan.

ITALIAN HUMANISM

Origins

The humanism movement in Italy represented a return to the values, culture, people, and art of ancient Rome and Greece. Humanism emphasized the importance of people and human values in literature, art, education, science, and government. Humanism began in Italy and then spread throughout the rest of Europe.

The ancient cultures of Rome and Greece had not been completely forgotten during the Middle Ages. Greek and Roman writings had been saved and copied in monasteries and schools in many parts of Europe. People who were well educated knew about ancient history, Greek and Roman authors, heroic legends, and mythology.

Libraries of the time had collections of books that reflected the interest some scholars had in ancient times. These libraries contained ancient books on geography, on the art of war, and on architecture. Moreover, people who had traveled to Byzantium and other lands in the east came back with large numbers of books on many different subjects.

Despite the collapse of the Roman Empire and the cultural dominance of Christianity, important elements of classical thought, especially Roman thought, were passed down through the centuries. It was this body of knowledge that formed the basis of Italian humanism.

One of the first humanists was Petrarch (1304–1374), an Italian born in Tuscany who later lived in Avignon. Petrarch was a famous poet and scholar who studied the Latin writers of ancient Rome. Petrarch wrote in the original classical Latin, not the Latin commonly in use in his time in the universities. Other scholars followed Petrarch's example and studied other classical texts in monastery libraries. These humanists believed that the ancient texts were not only examples of good writing style but also guides to living.

At first, the humanists concentrated on the rediscovery of the classical world through the study of Roman history, literature, and art. The earliest humanists such as Petrarch and Boccaccio tried to learn Greek so they could study Greek culture, which they believed served as the foundation of Roman culture. Through the study of ancient Greek, humanism reached its highest achievements. The work of Lorenzo Valla serves as a good example.

After having completed a study of the Latin used by Cicero, the great Roman writer, Valla, thanks to his knowledge of Greek, translated the Bible from the Greek versions. Valla revealed how the original text of the Bible had been changed over the years.

Some humanists were given political appointments. The wealth of their knowledge was considered a vital asset to their political and moral duties in the society they represented. By this time, with the blending of the academic world and the political world, the nature of humanism began to change. Writers now seem interested in producing works that glorified the political leaders of the various Italian states.

Italian Art

Humanism had a profound impact on Italian art. Religious themes had dominated art in the Middle Ages, confining the development of art into very strict and stylized channels. Just as humanism in literature emphasized the importance of humanity and classical values and forms, so did the art of the fifteenth century.

In painting and sculpture, each theme, including those of a religious nature, was approached from a human point of view. Great emphasis was placed on anatomy, perspective, proportion, and the use of color. The human body was studied in great detail.

During the Middle Ages, artists had a dual vision of art. They followed the dictates of religion on one hand and the dictates of a strict artistic style on the other. Art in the Middle Ages was considered a craft and was tied to the church and to the guilds. As such, art was a very important part of the political life of the Italian cities. But as Italian cities and states came to be controlled by single families or leaders, the power of the guilds over art weakened. The princes and lords became great supporters of art, and artists became part of court life.

The world of art was not a closed society. Artistic works such as sculptures and new buildings were often created in full view of the public, which discussed the merits and faults of the new art with great vigor and interest. When the dome of Santa Maria del Fiore in Florence was designed by the architect Brunelleschi, the citizens passionately discussed its merits and faults.

Humanism from 1450 to 1500

Compared with the previous fifty years, the art and literature of the second half of the fifteenth century appeared fairly stagnant. As writers became more involved with political leaders, their works became less intellectual and were written to please the prince or lord who supported the writer.

These princes and lords found it fashionable to show interest in literature and in writers. Literature became elitist and aristocratic. Works like Boiardo's *Orlando in Love* or Arioso's *Orlando the Furius* were reserved for the members of the prince's court. Praising cultural pleasures of the intellect was in style.

This brought about a split in the world of Italian culture. On one side, writers produced pleasant, undemanding literature for the courts of the political leaders. On the other side, universities and other schools encouraged serious thought and writing. In the meantime, common citizens showed more interest in the newly developing theater.

Above: This plan for the Basilica of St. Peter's in Vatican City is laid out in the form of a cross. The basilica was designed by Bramante, an Italian architect and painter who became Superintendent of Buildings for Pope Julius II. Work on rebuilding St. Peter's began in April 1506 but was not finished by Bramante, and his design underwent radical alterations. However, the innovations developed by Bramante were revolutionary enough to give new direction to Italian architecture.

Right: This scene shows the architect Brunelleschi checking the work being done on Santa Maria del Fiore Cathedral in Florence. The construction of public buildings in Italian cities became an occasion for citizens to discuss the projects and plans of the architects. During this time, the ties between artists and common people were very strong.

ECONOMIC GROWTH IN ITALY

The Links Between Commerce and Credit

As trade increased in the fourteenth and fifteenth centuries, Italian merchants responded to the strong demand for credit and foreign currency needed to conduct business. The great Italian trading companies often served as banks, lending out money or creating credit for their customers. These companies operated through a dense network of branch offices in Italy, the rest of Europe, and the east. Peruzzi, a banking and trading house in Florence had thirteen branches throughout Europe.

These companies wanted to lend money at a profit, and the method they used was the bill of exchange. The company wrote a bill of exchange for a certain amount of money for a person who wanted to conduct business in a foreign city. The company issuing the bill of exchange anticipated that it would be paid back in foreign currency at the company's branch in the foreign city and that a profit would be made in the amount that was paid back.

A Shift in the Economic Balance of Europe

Trade in northern Europe, except for the cities in the Hanseatic League, was based primarily on agricultural products. Trade in the Nordic countries, such as Sweden and Norway, was based on fish, wood, and metals. The prices for these goods were traditionally low, and trade in these products suffered during times of crisis.

Trade in Italy and in those Mediterranean areas controlled by Italian commerce was based on luxury goods such as jewelry and silk, and other precious and rare items. Demand for these luxury items increased in northern Europe during the fourteenth and fifteenth centuries. Since the products the northern countries exported were not as valuable as the products imported, the difference had to be paid in precious metals, such as gold or silver.

The flow of precious metals to Italy increased throughout the fourteenth and fifteenth centuries, making the Italian merchants and cities among the richest in the world. This shift in the commercial balance of Europe provoked heated reactions from both England and the cities of the Hanseatic League. They accused the Italian merchants of fraud and often prevented these merchants from trading in areas under English or Hanseatic control.

The shift in the European economic balance was not the only reason why the economies of the countries in northern Europe were ruined.

Kingdoms and principalities lost enormous amounts of money because of the continuous wars they fought. The irony of the situation was that Italian merchants and producers benefited from these wars. Companies in Milan made fortunes manufacturing and exporting arms to the warring states, and Genoa and Venice hired out their fleets to France and England during the Hundred Years War.

All of these factors created a lack of money in northern Europe. This condition remained unchanged until the last half of the fifteenth century when gold and silver began flowing into the European economy first from mines in central Europe and then, more abundantly, from Spanish colonies in the Americas.

The Italian commercial companies did not always make a profit from their ventures. There was great risk involved in extending credit and investing in trading operations. Some companies went out of business during this time because they lent money to King Edward III of England to fight the Hundred Years War, and the king never paid back the loans.

But the failure of some companies tended to feed the expansion of others. The Medici, for example, developed a special relationship with the pope and often operated as intermediaries in collecting offerings to the church.

Venice prospered during this period thanks to its strong political ties to other states and to its strategic geographic location. Venice had strong ties to the Byzantine Empire and to other powers in the eastern Mediterranean. The Venetians increased their power when they defeated Genoa, their major rival, in 1381. Over the years, Venice used its economic well-being to increase its military strength, thus becoming a strong military force as well as a major trading power.

Despite its defeat by Venice, Genoa remained a major port for trade in the western Mediterranean, especially with the kingdoms of the Iberian Peninsula in Spain and Portugal. Milan also experienced considerable economic growth during this time, especially in the production of arms and armor.

All of Italy, however, did not enjoy economic prosperity. Cities away from the coast often had difficulty getting essential goods. Southern Italy, a large producer of grain crops, suffered greatly when the prices for grains dropped.

Top: A fourteenth century Venetian brooch decorated with precious gems and pearls.

This scene shows the Rialto Bridge in Venice. This part of the city was the hub of political power. The vast majority of Venice's commercial and economic activity took place in the area around the Rialto.

Hanseatic League ☐
Genoa ☐
Venice ■

Areas of
Commercial
Influence

25

REVOLUTIONARY HERESIES

Throughout the Middle Ages, the Roman Catholic church was challenged many times by reformers who opposed the church's teachings on certain points of theology or who thought the church was too powerful, too rich, and too corrupt. Those people who spoke out against the church or preached new or different Christian doctrines in opposition to what the church taught were often called heretics. The doctrines preached by these people were called heresies. Some heresies died natural deaths, but others were stamped out violently by the church. Heretics were usually excommunicated. At times, however, excommunication was not strong enough punishment, and some heretics were executed.

As a general rule, the heresies of the fourteenth and fifteenth centuries were more political and intellectual than the heresies of the past. The new heresies were more political because the religious ideas they presented were often mixed with a desire for governmental change. The heresies were more intellectual because the people who preached them were often scholars who had studied and taught at the universities. Two of the most important heretical movements of the time were those led by John Wycliffe in England and Jan Hus in Bohemia.

John Wycliffe

John Wycliffe (1330–1384) was a teacher at Oxford University and an advisor to the king of England. Wycliffe taught that the Bible was the only true source of faith and that each believer was able to understand Holy Scripture without having to rely on the church to explain what the Scriptures meant. Wycliffe also denied the importance of the sacraments and the superiority of priests over laymen.

Wycliffe's writings were very intellectual and dry, and not many people read them. Wycliffe's teachings, however, did inspire groups of roving scholars and priests called Lollards who traveled throughout England preaching Wycliffe's ideas. Many of these Lollards had graduated from Oxford where they had been influenced by Wycliffe's teachings. The Lollards preached direct interpretation of the Bible and came out against the established clergy. The Lollards were seen as a threat to both the king and the church, but it took several years for the king and the church to silence them.

This case contained the crown of Bohemia. Bohemia was linked politically and culturally to Germany, and both countries were part of the Holy Roman Empire. During the reign of Emperor Charles IV (1348–1378), Bohemia enjoyed a period of great development. The emperor chose to live in Prague, and the University of Prague became a meeting ground for German and Slavic cultures. Coexistence between the two cultures was not always peaceful, and the political links with Germany did not prevent the development of a Czech national identity. This feeling of Slavic unity grew stronger during the Hussite period when even the nobles sided against the emperor.

The illustration below shows the walled fortress on top of Mount Tabor, where the most radical faction of the Hussites met. The Taborites were too extreme for most Hussites and a clash between the two groups led to the defeat of the Taborites in 1434.

A Hussite seal

Jan Hus

Wycliffe's ideas became widespread in Bohemia. His major writings became known there around 1390. There were already active groups in Bohemia calling for reform in the church. This movement was led by popular preachers like Matteo di Janov, and the core of support for the movement came from professors and students at the University of Prague.

At this point Jan Hus (1369?–1415) came to the forefront. Hus, the son of peasants, had become a professor of theology at the University of Prague. Hus accepted only some of Wycliffe's ideas. He rejected Wycliffe's teachings about the sacraments, but supported Wycliffe's criticism of the church.

Although Hus was declared a heretic, his preaching was very popular among the lower classes, and he also had the support of the nobles and aristocracy. But neither the common people nor the aristocracy could help Hus when he was called before the Council of Constance in 1414 to explain his teachings. The Council condemned Hus to death.

The execution outraged the people of Bohemia, who rose up in protests against the Holy Roman emperor and the pope. The Hussites combined the idea of religious reform with that of national rebirth, and thereby gained the support of the local nobility and the middle classes. It took fifteen years for the emperor to restore order in Bohemia. For the first time, the ideas of a heretic had given rise to a movement capable of rousing a whole nation.

The Taborites

Mount Tabor was an armed fortress in Bohemia where the most radical branch of the Hussites met. These radicals had taken their name from the Mount Tabor mentioned in the Bible. The Taborites welcomed all types of heretics, and their more radical approach to reform precipitated a split from the more conservative Hussites of Prague. The conflict between the two groups grew violent, and the Hussites of Prague defeated the Taborites in 1434.

This scene shows Jan Hus explaining his theories to members of the Council of Constance who condemned Hus to death.

Hus was influenced by the writings of John Wycliffe, which became known in Bohemia around 1390. Wycliffe's teachings took root in a climate of moral and ecclesiastical reform led by popular preachers like Matteo di Janov. At the core of the movement were the professors and students at the University of Prague. Jan Hus, a son of peasants who rose to be Rector of the University of Prague, was a product of this environment. The relationship between the teachings of Hus and the political unrest within Czech society is one of the most interesting aspects of the Hussite movement. When the Council of Constance condemned Hus, all members of Czech society were enraged. The desire for religious reform and a deep sense of nationalism mingled together in the long struggle between Bohemia, the pope, and the Holy Roman emperor.

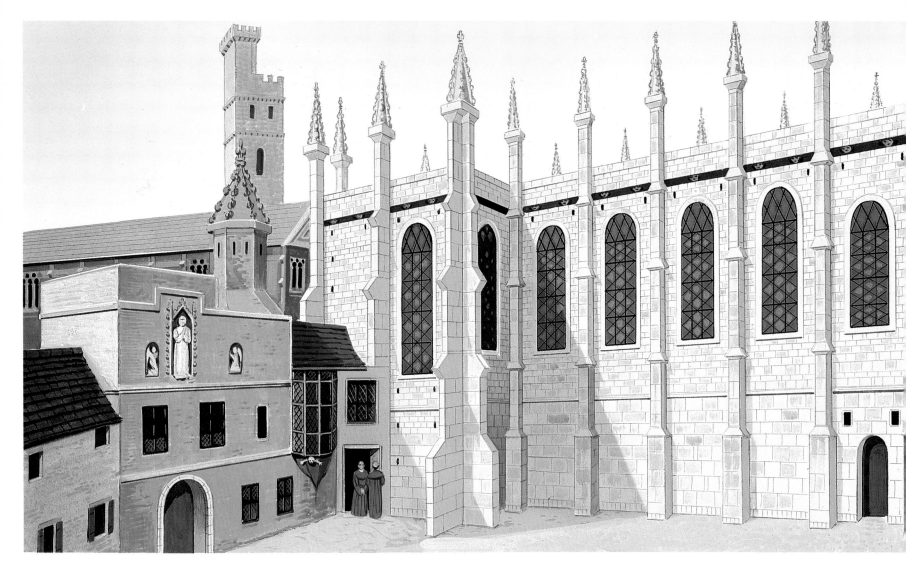

TROUBLES WITHIN THE CHURCH

Avignon and Rome

Between 1309 and 1377 the popes of the Catholic church lived in the French city of Avignon, not in Rome. The popes were forced to leave Rome due to the chaotic nature of Italian politics. This period was called the "Babylonian Captivity." During this period, the church underwent many changes. All of the popes were French, and they made the papacy into an efficient administrative organization. But this efficiency did not mask the differences between the pope and common believers.

In the past, ecumenical councils, or gatherings of local or national church leaders, had met to discuss their problems. This was no longer so. In addition to being removed from ordinary members of the church, the popes often gave influential positions within the church to their own relatives. The popes paid these relatives very well and often became involved in power struggles between different groups. The popes had enormous powers but seemed unable to carry out their real role as religious leaders. This failure caused the lack of confidence in the popes to increase.

In 1377 Pope Gregory XI decided to return the papacy to Rome. By this action, Gregory hoped to restore part of the church's lost prestige and to satisfy many Catholics who felt the pope's true home was in the Holy City. Many of the church's cardinals opposed the move.

The Great Schism

After Pope Gregory XI died, the French cardinals chose Clement VII as pope and installed him in Avignon. A second pope, Urban VI, took office in Rome. This caused a split, or schism, in the Catholic church that is known historically as the Great Schism.

This division lasted about forty years and added greatly to the atmosphere of crisis in the late Middle Ages. The schism had political as well as religious ramifications. Italy, Germany, and England supported Urban VI and his successors, while the popes in Avignon were supported by France, Scotland, the kingdoms of the Iberian Peninsula, and Naples.

The schism, which started as a split within the papacy, soon became a crisis throughout the whole church. Neither of the rival popes could gain the upper hand, and the failure of

the papacy was seen as a symptom of deeper problems within the church. There obviously was a need for reform, and certain intellectuals and church leaders thought reform could be achieved by reviving the ecumenical councils.

The Councils

The first council was held at the Italian city of Pisa in 1409. During the meeting of this council, both rival popes were removed from office, and a third pope was elected. This solution proved a total failure because now the church had three popes.

Another council was held at Constance between 1414 and 1418. The Council of Constance declared that it had authority over church affairs greater than any pope, even in matters of doctrine. The council failed to eliminate the schism completely or to bring about much needed church reforms.

At first the rulers of the most powerful countries and states in Europe had supported the councils, but now they lost interest. The goal of the sovereigns had been to get more control over the church in the lands they ruled, but the councils did not bring this about.

The rulers decided that it was easier to deal with a weak and divided papacy than with a single powerful pope. In 1438 Charles VII of France issued the Pragmatic Sanction, a decree that limited control of the papacy over the church in France.

The Consequences of the Schism

The Great Schism further weakened a papacy that had already been hurt by the residency of the popes in Avignon. Christianity was split by having two or even three popes at once. The pope's prestige suffered enormously, and the councils had tried to set themselves above any pope. To overcome these forces within the church, the popes had to search for support among the political leaders of Europe, often giving these leaders special privileges.

The schism was finally ended with the election of Pope Martin V by the Council of Constance in 1417. The entire church agreed to accept Martin as the one and only pope. After the schism, the popes tended to behave more like princes, especially in their control over the Papal States in Italy.

Throughout the Middle Ages, the popes had both temporal and spiritual powers. Through their spiritual powers, they were the religious leaders of the church. Through their temporal powers, they were the political leaders over the lands of the Papal States in Italy. To protect both powers, the popes after the schism paid great attention to their diplomatic and military roles in ruling their state.

This scene shows a Faculty of Theology where religious themes and ideas were discussed by scholars, students, and priests. The Great Schism (1377) divided the Roman Catholic church for about forty years and was one of the major causes of the crisis within the church during the late Middle Ages. The schism began as a split within the papacy but later caused divisions within the entire church.

The anguish caused by the crisis in the Roman Catholic church was widely felt throughout Europe. Having two or three popes confused the common people and made them feel insecure. This led to a constant fear of death, which was ever present in the daily lives of the faithful. This illustration shows this fear of death. Artists of the time often painted terrible scenes of death, or scenes where death triumphs over all. (Fifteenth Century, Haute Loire, France)

EUROPEAN ECONOMY AND SOCIETY IN THE FIFTEENTH CENTURY

Economic and social conditions changed gradually in Europe during the fifteenth century. These changes had their roots in the economic crisis and social conditions of the fourteenth century, but the recovery in the fifteenth century took on a nature of its own. It was during this period of revival that the foundations of present-day Europe were laid down.

New Forms of Agriculture

Agriculture in the fourteenth century had centered around raising grain crops. As prices for these crops fell, farmlands were abandoned or used for the production of new crops such as grapes and flax. This trend continued in the fifteenth century. More land was used to raise flax, grapes, fruit, and olives. Abandoned farmlands were slowly reclaimed.

Breeding livestock became more common. Raising sheep was especially profitable thanks to the development of the weaving industry. In prior centuries, raising livestock had taken place in the wild. Animals were allowed to roam freely in the woods. The number of animals per breeder was never very high. This all changed in the fifteenth century. Raising sheep or cattle became highly organized. Animals were branded and grouped into herds. Land was set aside for grazing, and a tax was levied on livestock.

The Enclosures

The development of enclosures, lands fenced off for grazing, is an important concept in the history of European agriculture. Enclosures cut off lands peasants had used for farming, thereby forcing the peasants to leave their homes and move to cities. This migration changed the social nature of Europe.

Breeding livestock on a large scale requires large amounts of land. Large flocks of sheep are difficult to manage if allowed to roam freely. This is why it is necessary to fence off areas of land where the flocks will graze. In the first half of the fifteenth century, major English breeders began to enclose large areas of land for their sheep.

These enclosures took farmland from the peasants, who, having no other way to make a living, abandoned their villages and moved to larger towns and cities. Since these peasants were unskilled and very poor, they accepted any work they could get.

The introduction of enclosures was slower on the European continent. In the fifteenth century, however, hedges and walls dividing open areas became increasingly common, changing the look and customs of the countryside.

The use of woodlands also changed at this time. During previous centuries, woods and forests were a source of food for peasants. Hunting, fishing, and gathering wild fruit helped peasants survive famines. Gradually, throughout the fifteenth and sixteenth centuries, the people who actually owned the woods and forests reserved them for private use. The freedom to hunt was limited, and cutting wood or grazing animals was forbidden.

New Trades and Occupations

New techniques for producing goods such as cloth and clothing near the end of the thirteenth century led to greater and more varied production of these goods. During the fourteenth century, differences between products destined for the rich and those produced for the poor became more apparent. Until this time, the clothes of the rich were usually distinguished by the use of expensive colors, like red, or by adding fur. But in the fourteenth and fifteenth centuries, clothing for the rich became much different from that of the poor. Fashion became a sign of social status, and clothes for the rich were distinguished by extravagant styles and the use of fine fabrics.

The demand for products of different styles, quality, and price enlarged the market for these goods and was one of the causes for the expansion of trades and crafts. Workers were plentiful in both the cities and countryside, and the textile industry growth benefited both types.

The production of linen, for example, required some tasks be carried out in the countryside where flax is grown. Harvesting the flax, rinsing it in running water, and drying it were all done in the open air and thus easier to do in the countryside. The flax was then transported into towns or cities where it was dyed, woven into cloth, and finally made into clothing.

Small villages sprang up around the walls of a town or city. These villages were supported by work given by businesses in the city or town. Work began to be divided by the complexity of the tasks. Workers in the countryside performed simpler tasks, while workers in the cities or towns did more complicated ones.

Right: This scene shows silver mining in Bohemia. Mining boomed during the fifteenth century. Iron, especially, was in great demand for making arms.

Fashion began to demonstrate social status. Tailors made special clothes for nobles and members of the middle class. These clothes were made of fine materials, and their styles reflected the social position of the people who wore them.

Textile production was carried out partly in the countryside and partly in the towns. This picture shows how materials were dyed, a task done in town, where the more difficult technological tasks were carried out. People in rural areas became increasingly involved with textile production but were usually given simpler jobs.

This scene shows a glimpse of daily life in Innsbruck, Austria. The illustration was inspired by the notebook of Albrecht Dürer, the German painter who left the world wonderful evidence of his travels.

THE ROLE OF REGIONAL STATES AND CITIES WITHIN THE HOLY ROMAN EMPIRE

The Weakness of the Emperor

The Holy Roman Empire was the dominant power in central Europe during the Middle Ages. The empire, sometimes referred to as Germany or the German Empire, was actually a collection of more than three hundred separate towns, cities, and states owing allegiance to the emperor. The name, Germany, was more a geographic term than a political entity.

The empire was composed of many different groups of people, each with their own traditions. The western part of the empire was influenced by France, and its inhabitants spoke French. The eastern parts of the empire had Slavic traditions, and the inhabitants there spoke a variety of Slavic languages. The heart of the empire, however, stretching from the Rhine River on the west to the Oder River on the east, and from the Baltic Sea on the north to the Brenner Pass on the south, was thoroughly Germanic in nature.

The office of emperor was not hereditary, but elective. When one emperor died, the rulers of the various states and cities within the empire elected a new emperor. In 1356 Emperor Charles IV issued a decree called the Golden Bull under which he revised the election of emperors. Charles said that from 1356 on, the emperors would be elected only by three German church leaders and four local rulers. These special electors would receive certain privileges usually reserved for kings, such as the right to mint coins.

During the fourteenth and fifteenth centuries, the electors tended to choose emperors who posed no threat to the powers the electors themselves had. It was hardly by chance that the elected emperors always came from territories far away from the heart of the empire, places like Luxembourg, Bohemia, and Austria. This policy tended to weaken the authority of the emperor. These emperors were not always totally ineffective, but they did tend to concentrate on problems within their own states rather than on the problems of the empire as a whole.

One Empire with Many Centers

The almost king-like authority with which the electors ruled their territories was imitated by other princes and church leaders, and by cities within the empire. Each of the more than three hundred self-governing territories within the empire had its own diet, or ruling assembly. Each territory also had its own capital, judicial system, and army.

The presence of many political centers was not the only sign of imperial weakness. Just as important was the fact that there were no general rules in effect throughout the empire regulating economic development. Without imperial control, many cities within the empire established their own policies. Economic growth within the empire gave birth to self-ruling groups, or leagues of cities, such as the Hanseatic League, the Swabian League, and a league of commercial centers along the Rhine River.

The Rural Economy

Strong differences were also present in the rural areas throughout the empire. In Saxony, free peasants commonly owned their own lands, while in other parts of the empire, peasants were still obligated to the local lords. In the northwestern part of the empire, commercial links with Flemish, Dutch, and English markets gave rise to the growth of large prosperous livestock farms.

Almost everywhere, the riches of the cities spilled into the countryside. Crafts, merchants, and important financiers invested part of their profits in the rural areas.

Attempts to Reform the Empire

Under Emperor Maximilian I (1493–1519) some attempts were made to reform the empire. Maximilian created the Imperial Court of Law that, in time, was used to settle disputes between different lords. For the first time a tax was passed to cover the expenses of war. In 1512 the empire was divided into ten districts ruled over by two princes who had the right to collect taxes and recruit an army. These measures did not aim at transforming the empire into a modern state, but simply tried to guarantee the empire would function more smoothly on a daily basis.

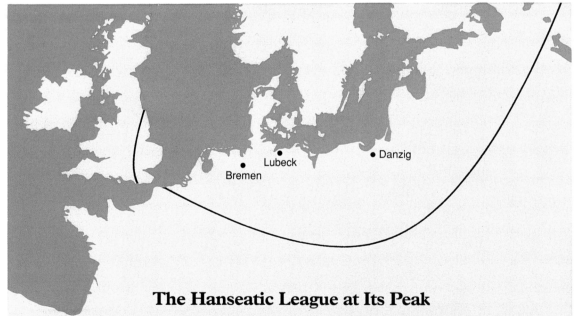

The Hanseatic League at Its Peak

This map shows the area dominated by the Hanseatic League. The cities within this area were actively engaged in commerce and grouped themselves together to form the league.

During the first half of the fifteenth century, this great association was at the height of its power, and it controlled all trade in the North Sea. In 1375 seventy-seven cities belonged to the Hanseatic League. By 1450, the number had increased to two hundred. The Hanseatic League also controlled trade routes within the empire as far west as Cologne. Merchants from the League traveled up the Rhine River as far as the Alps. So many Hanseatic merchants did business in Italy, that they were given their special commercial areas in Venice along with a covered marketplace called the German Warehouse.

ART AND THOUGHT IN THE FLEMISH AND GERMAN WORLD

The Search for New Forms of Spirituality

People who lived in Europe during the fourteenth and fifteenth centuries were obsessed by the question of salvation — saving their souls. The wars, the famines, the plague, the revolts and the schism in the Roman Catholic church cast a shadow of doubt on beliefs once held as certain. The world had become more insecure, more difficult to understand, and more threatening. Many of the faithful felt that performing good works and observing the sacraments were simply not enough to satisfy their religious needs.

The old medieval society was changing, and many people felt the desire to live their religion in a more personal way. A renewed desire for religious education was typical in the fourteenth and fifteenth centuries, and the church responded to this need in different ways. Often the clergy — priests, nuns, and monks — were not prepared to teach Christian culture, but, in time, the church found ways to educate the faithful. From the fourteenth century on, schools organized by the church improved enormously in the way religion was taught. Essays on meditation and prayer were written in the languages spoken by common people.

In the fourteenth century, a new emphasis on devotion spread from Flanders and Holland into Germany. For devout Christians,

belonging to a church no longer meant simply attending religious services but also that one's faith should be present in daily life. For this reason, much attention was given to prayer and to meditating on Sacred Scriptures. Followers of this doctrine usually lived in cities and dedicated most of the time they were not working to this new "modern devotion."

Prayer, reading Sacred Scripture together, and collective examination of conscience created an austere way of life for these people and set them apart from other Christians. They were dedicated to preaching but were convinced that the best way they could help others was through prayer and by setting good examples with their lives.

These groups took special care in educating their children and had schools where children were brought up according to the new principles of the devotion. Many diaries, letters, and manuals were written in order to share with others the religious experiences these people had. The most important of these works is *The Imitation of Christ* written by Thomas à Kempis. It is one of the best examples of late medieval Christian thought, a form of thought that searched for salvation through a life of austerity, meditation, and prayer.

New Styles of Art

A new style of art began to evolve in Flanders in the beginning of the fifteenth

century. Flemish artists developed a more realistic style, and painters moved toward a more sensitive treatment of light in their paintings. Jan van Eyck (1380?–1441) is considered the initiator of this new school of Flemish painting.

The interiors of rooms in van Eyck's paintings were depicted in great detail, and everyday objects were often present in his paintings. The people in van Eyck's paintings always seem very serious and impassive, like the subjects of his painting entitled *Portrait of Giovanni Arnolfini and His Wife*.

Van Eyck's *The Adoration of the Mystic Lamb* was finished in 1412 and is considered one of the masterpieces of Flemish art. The twelve canvases of this work show sacred scenes and figures, detailed landscapes, and portraits.

Van Eyck's skill with light and color so impressed his contemporaries that he was long believed to be the inventor of oil painting. In reality, van Eyck had perfected an already existing technique that encouraged the reflection of light in a painting. Van Eyck's attention to detail, his use of color and light, and the amazing depth of his portraits had a great influence on all European art.

Albrecht Dürer

Albrecht Dürer was a German artist born in Nuremberg in 1471. In his work, Dürer seems to have captured the anguish that tormented the German people at this time.

Dürer spent several years in Italy and Flanders where he learned much from the Italian painter Andrea Mantegna and from van Eyck. Dürer began as a portraitist but then branched out into other forms of art. During his travels, he created his first lithographs. Dürer's work began to be appreciated after he finished eight xylographs, or woodcuts, on the subject of the Apocalypse.

Dürer was inspired by deep religious sentiment and the growing anguish of German Christians is evident in his works entitled *Apocalypse* and *St. Jerome*.

A portrait of Erasmus of Rotterdam by Albrecht Dürer. Erasmus was a great humanist who hoped that direct examination of the Holy Scriptures and studying the works of the Fathers of the church would lead to reform within the Roman Catholic church.

A double-bottomed wooden tankard, decorated in silver. (End of the tenth century, Karlsruhe, Badisches Landesmuseum)

This scene shows the austere atmosphere in which followers of the "new devotion" lived. This kind of life set these people apart from other Christians. After a day's work was over, they met to read the Sacred Scriptures and other religious texts.

CHANGES IN NORTHERN AND CENTRAL EUROPE DURING THE FIFTEENTH CENTURY

Control of the Baltic Trade

In the beginning of the fifteenth century, the Hanseatic League monopolized trade in the Baltic and North seas. But toward the middle of the fifteenth century, two new powers, first the Dutch and then the English, challenged the power of the league.

The league did not present a united front against the Dutch and English because there were constant disagreements among the individual cities in the league. Only two cities remained strong, Riga at the mouth of the Dvina River and Danzig (now called Gdansk) at the mouth of the Vistula River. Both cities remained important because they controlled the flow of trade up both rivers to the grain producing regions of northern Europe.

The Dutch were swift to seize the trading opportunities left open by the demise of the Hanseatic League. Dutch ships were loaded at Bruges, Antwerp, Calais, and Amsterdam with goods to transport into the Baltic countries where they were exchanged for wax, grain, linen, and wool. English ships also took part in this trade, a sign of the future when England would be a leading sea power. Antwerp (in Belgium) served as a major port for the English, and the city boomed during this period.

Hungary Before the Turkish Conquest

At the beginning of the fourteenth century, the branch of the Angevin family that ruled southern Italy also ruled Hungary. The Angevins were interested only in furthering their own family interests in Hungary, which they did through a number of rather complicated dynastic intermarriages with other royal families.

The Angevins surrounded themselves with Italian artists and intellectuals, thereby increasing the influence of Western culture in Hungary. The Angevins also tried to reduce the power of the local lords but failed to do so. The Angevin dynasty ruled until 1386 when the crown passed to Sigismund, king of Bohemia and Holy Roman emperor.

Throughout the early part of the fifteenth century, Hungary was Europe's eastern-most outpost of Christianity against the Ottoman Turks. The Hungarian aristocracy took a part in the European offensive against the Turks which ended with the Europeans being soundly

A picture of the port of Antwerp in the sixteenth century based on a sketch by Dürer. Between the fourteenth and sixteenth centuries, Antwerp became an important center of trade, as the ports of the Hanseatic League declined.

defeated at the Battle of Varna in 1444. The Hungarian forces recovered and were able to stop the Turkish advance at Belgrade in 1456.

Matthias Corvinus became king of Hungary in 1458. Under Corvinus, Hungary conquered a string of principalities stretching from Bosnia to Moravia. When Corvinus died, the Hungarian crown passed to Vladislav, king of Bohemia, thereby creating a stronger tie with the German world.

Poland

In the early years of the fourteenth century, Poland began to reestablish itself as a strong power in eastern Europe. Like much of Europe at the time, Poland was a collection of principalities often at war with one another. Under Wladyslaw I, many of these principalities were brought back under central control.

To further strengthen the royal position, Wladyslaw's son, Casimir III, created a new class of nobles loyal to the king. Casimir died in 1370 leaving no male heirs. He was succeeded by Louis I of Hungary. When Louis died, his daughter, Jadwiga, became queen of Poland.

Queen Jadwiga married Wladyslaw Jagiello of Lithuania, uniting the two countries. The Teutonic Knights, enemies of Poland for almost a hundred years, declared war on the Poles and were soundly defeated at the Battle of Tannenberg in 1410.

Under Casimir IV, Poland reached the high point of its resurgence as a great power. Casimir gave the Teutonic Knights back some

of the territories they had lost, but denied them access to the Baltic Sea. In an attempt to reinforce his authority over the nobles, the king called together local assemblies to confirm his decisions. Casimir also assumed direct control of internal Polish trade, taking it away from the merchants of the Hanseatic League.

Casimir tried to extend Poland's influence into Bohemia and Hungary. But Casimir's ambitions died when he did. As the Polish nobility regained their former political strength, it showed far more interest in the benefits of trade with Germany than with extending the power of the Polish rulers. In 1505 the nobles managed to obtain from the king an agreement that said the king could not take action on any decision unless the nobles approved.

ENGLAND AND FRANCE AFTER 1450

England

At the end of the Hundred Years War, England found itself relatively isolated from events on the European continent. The war had weakened the traditional forms of order in the kingdom, and under King Henry VI, the monarchy lost its ability to influence politics. Probably, one of the chief reasons for this was the king's personality. Henry was weak, mentally ill, and therefore unable to deal with the demands of the lords or to keep control of the government. The kingdom itself was structured in such a way that local lords were the dominant powers in their respective areas.

All these elements helped bring about the internal struggles that shook the kingdom during the last half of the fourteenth century.

Historians usually refer to these struggles as the War of the Roses. The name refers to the wars fought between the houses of Lancaster and York in their struggle for the English throne. Both families used a rose—one red, one white—as their symbols.

The first skirmishes in these wars were fought between powerful nobles over who should control the throne. Henry VI was defeated in 1460, and Edward of York became King Edward IV. Edward IV failed to bring peace to the country, but he did keep power for over twenty years and helped restore the administration of justice and the consolidation of finances.

The dynastic struggle continued in the northern part of England, the house of Lancaster continued to show furious resistance.

Even after being defeated, pockets of armed opposition to the Yorkist king remained. Consequently, the kingdom, although not devastated by outright war, suffered through a period of disorder, minor battles, and troubled government.

Edward IV was succeeded by his brother Richard III who lost the crown to the exiled Henry Tudor, earl of Richmond. Supported by the French, Henry landed in Wales in 1485, where he got support from the Welsh lords. He gradually succeeded in overcoming the people's lack of confidence in his bid for the throne.

The War of the Roses ended with the reign of Henry VII. He was a strong king who made able use of the traditional workings of the English monarchy. Henry VII formed his

After one hundred years of war, life went more or less back to normal for France, at least for the nobility. This scene shows a noble family enjoying a trip on a river, one of the most typical pastimes for members of the aristocracy at the time.

Council of State around a small group of men he had brought with him from France, but also included members of the English aristocracy and of the church. The Council of State had far-reaching powers and soon became the instrument through which the king ruled.

Financially speaking, the monarchy supported itself with traditional forms of taxation and with money donated by the aristocracy to show their support of the king. The administration of justice was reinforced and placed under the direction of a royal court called the Star Chamber.

With this widespread reorganization of the English government, Henry VII was able to consolidate the power of his family, and he is rightly considered the founder of the Tudor dynasty. When he died in 1509, he left his son Henry VIII in a strong financial position, with a council that worked well, and an efficient government structure in place.

France

As the victor in the Hundred Years War, France increased in size during the second half of the fifteenth century. The king's authority, however, was not uniform throughout the country. Brittany in the west and Burgundy in the east existed more or less independently of the crown.

In other regions, provincial nobles actively prevented rapid unification of the country. The Bourbons possessed an enormous duchy in central France. The dukes of Valois and Orléans ruled over their territories, and the region around Avignon remained under the pope's rule. There were also regions such as Normandy that governed themselves.

Nor did France have a true capital. Paris was the center for certain departments of the government, but it was not the permanent capital. The king spent just as much time living in

castles along the Loire River as he did living in the Louvre in Paris.

The strong position of the nobles made the country politically unstable, and Louis XI (1423–1483) faced considerable opposition. The situation flared into civil war in 1465. The king was able to reassert his power but not strong enough to defeat the forces under the duke of Burgundy.

Toward the end of the fifteenth century, France began to turn its attention toward Mediterranean lands. In 1481 the region of Provence became part of France. But the king continued to look farther afield at places where there were untold riches and a chance to fight the forces of Islam. Nobles with a taste for adventure and merchants looking for new trade routes were only too ready to follow the desires of the king. When Charles VIII became king, the Mediterranean lands, especially Italy, became the focal point of French politics.

CHANGES ALONG THE RHINE

The coat of arms of the dukes of Burgundy.

The Duchy of Burgundy

France was so slow in reducing self-rule in some of the provinces, that the independence of some parts of the country actually increased. This was especially true in Burgundy, where, by the end of the fourteenth century, the duke of Burgundy's power spread over much of the territory between the mouth of the Rhine River and Geneva.

Philip the Good (1396–1467), duke of Burgundy, gained control over a large part of Flanders and other areas destined eventually to become the Low Countries. When these lands, and others, were added to Burgundy's control, the duchy became so large, and with so many cultural and economic differences, that Philip was forced to decentralize his government.

Four administrative centers were chosen: Dijon, Ghent, Brussels, and The Hague. Local politics were intense within the duchy, and Philip was wise enough to use these cities to help him govern. Other signs of Philip's originality as a ruler was the creation of one of the most famous orders of European knights, the Order of the Golden Fleece. Philip's encouragement of artistic expression reflected the character of the times.

Charles the Bold (1467–1477)

During the second half of the fifteenth century, the political life of Burgundy was marked by further attempts to gain territory. Duke Charles the Bold tried to capture Liege, a self-governing principality headed by a bishop. He hoped to control the independent lands that lay between the northern and southern parts of Burgundy. These lands consisted of scattered political units such as smaller duchies, cities, and territories belonging to the church. For a brief period, Charles managed to unify these territories, but in 1477 he was defeated and killed in a war with the duke of Lorraine, who was allied to the Swiss and Strasbourg.

Charles left a daughter, Mary, who married Maximilian I, a member of the Hapsburg family who went on to become a Holy Roman emperor. Through this marriage, the Hapsburg family extended its power in Europe, despite France's efforts to prevent this.

Following the policy of matrimonial and dynastic alliances so typical of the Hapsburgs, Philip, the son of Mary and Maximilian, married Joanna of Castile (1496), who became heir to the combined Spanish kingdoms of Aragon and Castile. Their son Charles, born in Ghent in 1500, was linked to several ruling families in

Europe, a fact that was to lead the Hapsburgs to the domination of European politics for a long time.

The Swiss Confederation

To the south of Burgundy, toward the Alps, the Swiss Confederation slowly began to take shape. This confederation grew powerful enough to become a deciding factor in the development of a vast region stretching from Lombardy to the Upper Rhine River.

The nucleus of the Swiss Confederation was formed at the end of the thirteenth century. It was composed of village communities organized by peasant-farmers, originally from southern Germany. This group of communities broke away from Hapsburg rule in 1315 and was rapidly joined by other towns and cities. In 1394 a peace treaty negotiated with the Hapsburgs gave the confederation an opportunity to expand its territory beyond the Alps. This expansion, for the most part, took place toward the south and was halted by Filippo Maria Visconti, duke of Milan, who defeated the Swiss in 1422.

The Swiss struggled to maintain their independence from the Hapsburgs. In theory Swiss lands belonged to the Holy Roman Empire, but when Maximilian I was crowned emperor, the confederation refused to acknowledge him as its ruler. By the end of the fifteenth century, the confederation was independent, although the influence of the empire would be felt for several decades.

The Swiss Confederation continued to expand during the first years of the sixteenth century. Eventually, Swiss expansion was halted, preventing the creation of a strong state perched on the Alps but spreading down into Italy.

This illustration shows the *Hotel de Dieu* in Beaune built by the dukes of Burgundy. The *Hotel de Dieu* was a charitable institution serving as a hospital and refuge for the poor. The most striking feature of this beautiful building is the contrast between its magnificent style and the use to which it was put.

NEW DEVELOPMENTS ON THE IBERIAN PENINSULA

Throughout the fifteenth century, major changes took place in the Iberian Peninsula kingdoms of Portugal, Aragon, and Castile. These changes would have long-lasting, major effects on the history of both Europe and the rest of the world.

By the end of the fifteenth century, Portugal had already exploited its geographical position on the Atlantic Ocean to establish itself as the exchange point of commerce between the North Sea and the Mediterranean Sea. Portugal's solid government together with its lively trade initiatives made it easy for the country to grasp the opportunity of exploring Africa. With the approval and support of the monarchy, Portuguese ships began to search along the coasts of Africa for a water route to India.

In addition to Portugal, the two most important kingdoms on the Iberian Peninsula were Aragon and Castile. The ruling family of Aragon had already extended its political and commercial influences in the Mediterranean by conquering the southern part of Italy and the islands of Sicily and Sardinia. The royal houses of Castile and Aragon were united through marriage and the combined forces of both kingdoms were powerful enough to defeat the kingdom of Granada, the last Muslim kingdom on the peninsula.

The Creation of the Kingdom of Spain

The ruling families of Castile and Aragon were united through the marriage of Isabella of Castile and Ferdinand of Aragon in 1469. The last of the Muslim forces in Spain were defeated at the Battle of Granada in 1492. After Isabella died in 1504, Ferdinand governed all the possessions belonging to both Castile and Aragon.

With the union of Castile and Aragon, a new single state, Spain, made its appearance on the European scene. The kingdom of Spain was a complex reality that would channel its energy toward the Americas, the Mediterranean Sea, and Europe as a whole.

The traditional political focus of the house of Aragon had been the Mediterranean, especially Italy. The kingdom of Spain maintained this tradition. Isabella and Ferdinand also developed strong relationships with the dukes of Burgundy and the ruling Hapsburg family of the Holy Roman empire. All these policies put Spain on a collision course with France, which was trying to restrain the power of the Hapsburgs and the dukes of Burgundy. France also had an interest in Italy, which, because of its riches, its geographical position, and its internal political weakness, tempted both Spain and France to become involved with its ruling factions.

Iberian Society

During the reign of Ferdinand and Isabella, both the cities and the nobles of Spain contributed to the centralization of power around the ruling couple. In this way, a certain balance was reached among the strongest forces of Spanish society.

The support given to the crown by the cities and nobles was richly rewarded. The *hermandad,* or League of Cities, became the government body responsible for internal law and order in Spain. The fertile lands of Granada were doled out to the nobles. Many nobles also received important government positions. It was therefore the nobles, or *hildagos,* who formed the core of the new Spain.

The Results of the "Reconquista" Spirit

The *Reconquista* spirit, the idea of ridding Spain of non-Spanish peoples, grew in strength during this period of Spain's history. Thus one of the most valuable aspects of medieval Spain was lost; its ability to welcome and absorb different cultures.

Because of this *Reconquista* spirit, any Muslims who remained in Spain after the defeat at Granada were forced to become Christians. Jewish residents of Spain were persecuted and exiled if they, too, did not convert. Through the Spanish Inquisition, the monarchy and the church tried to silence all those who were not Roman Catholic and faithful to the crown. The opinions of the monarchy, and, therefore, of the new nation, appeared more important at the moment than a truly Christian way of life.

Many important leaders of the church, like Father Bartolomé de Las Casas, soon realized the horror of such an attitude, especially when the Spanish began their conquest of the Americas. In his missionary work, Las Casas took an approach totally different from that of the *Reconquista*.

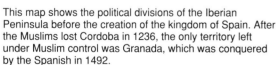

This scene takes place in the *Piazza dei Re*, the King's Square, in Barcelona, and shows Ferdinand and Isabella passing through an excited crowd of citizens from all walks of life.

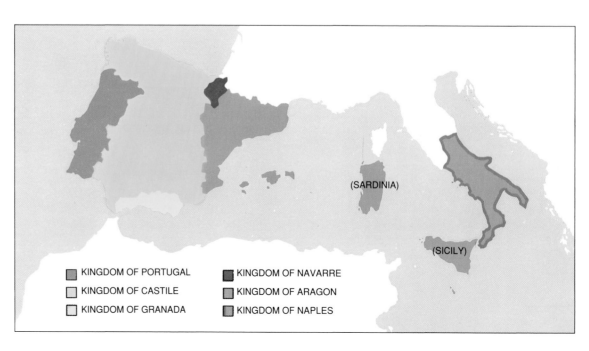

This map shows the political divisions of the Iberian Peninsula before the creation of the kingdom of Spain. After the Muslims lost Cordoba in 1236, the only territory left under Muslim control was Granada, which was conquered by the Spanish in 1492.
Portugal was an independent kingdom and important commercially because it was the exchange point for trade between the North Sea and the Mediterranean Sea.
In the fourteenth century the monarchy of Castile had tried to assert its power over the nobles but failed. The nobility and the church reinforced their control over the crown.
The kingdom of Aragon, which included Catalonia and Valencia, conquered southern Italy. The rise of Aragon's influence in the eastern Mediterranean favored the commercial development of the Catalonian cities such as Barcelona.

(SARDINIA)

(SICILY)

■ KINGDOM OF PORTUGAL   ■ KINGDOM OF NAVARRE

□ KINGDOM OF CASTILE   ■ KINGDOM OF ARAGON

□ KINGDOM OF GRANADA   ■ KINGDOM OF NAPLES

THE RENAISSANCE

Sixteenth Century Italy

During the first two decades of the sixteenth century, a new generation of Italian artists changed the world of art forever. Among these artists were Leonardo da Vinci, Michelangelo Buonarroti, and Raphael Sanzio.

Few personalities have impressed their contemporaries and future generations as much as Leonardo da Vinci (1452–1519). Leonardo defined himself as universal man, a man with many talents and an interest in everything. For Leonardo, scientific research and artistic composition went hand in hand. They offered two complimentary approaches to understanding the laws of nature and the universe.

Leonardo began his career as an artist in Florence, where he served as an apprentice to Andrea del Verrochio. He later moved to Milan, then back to Florence, and eventually to Rome. In 1515 he moved to Amboise, France, at the request of the French king.

In his paintings, Leonardo eliminated sharp lines separating image and space. He achieved this extreme delicacy of atmospheric effects through his use of sky-blue backgrounds together with misty halos surrounding his human figures. This lack of sharp definition set Leonardo's work apart from the other works of Florentine art typical of the fifteenth century. Magnificent examples of his work are *The Virgin of the Rocks*, *The Last Supper*, *The Sacred Family*, and the *Mona Lisa*.

Michelangelo Buonarroti (1471–1564) led a tormented life and often abandoned projects when difficulties arose between himself and his patrons. Michelangelo worked in Rome, Florence, Venice, and Bologna.

In his sculpture the *Pietá*, Michelangelo expressed a deep sense of suffering, a suffering he also worked into the sculpture of *Moses*, which decorates the tomb of Pope Julius II. Michelangelo's frescoes in the Sistine Chapel in Rome took four years to complete and resulted in a masterpiece in which he totally broke away from the traditions of the classical world. Michelangelo's powerful and disturbing images often caused controversy among those of his contemporaries who preferred the grace and lightness of the painter Raphael's style.

Raphael Sanzio (1483–1520) was an artist whose work enjoyed prolonged success due to his use of symmetry, contrasts of color, and the clever manipulation of light. The popes especially liked Raphael's work and decorated their living quarters with it.

The Renaissance not only produced great artists, but also great writers. Among these, one of the most famous is Niccolò Machiavelli (1469–1527), a Florentine diplomat who wrote a fundamental text on politics entitled *The Prince*. In this book, Machiavelli described how a ruler should go about creating and ruling an ideal state. The methods he suggested were sometimes harsh.

The Renaissance Spreads

Many of the most important intellectuals and artists of the time flocked to Italy as disciples of the cultural revolution taking place there. The revolution in Italian culture soon spread over the Alps and into the rest of Europe.

Erasmus of Rotterdam (1469–1536) was a humanist who had studied Latin and Greek, and was an eloquent speaker. He was an ordained priest who traveled in Italy and was welcomed in London, Paris, and Basel (Switzerland), where he taught.

Erasmus was a man without prejudices. He accepted all cultural influences including those growing out of the Reformation (see page 57) and the ideas of Machiavelli. Although he did not leave the Roman Catholic church, he did not believe in Divine Grace, and he considered the sacraments as symbolic. Erasmus preferred a faith supported by reason.

France took longer to achieve a cultural revolution than Italy or England. This was probably due to the attitude of the universities in France which tended to be reluctant to allow changes. They slowed down the development of a more modern school of thought.

Changes in art were expressed in Germany through the works of Albrecht Dürer (1471–1538), who traveled in Italy. In his last works, *The Apocalypse* and *St. Jerome*, Dürer showed the growing anguish of the Christian world of his times, an anguish that eventually led to the Reformation.

The Gutenberg Printing Press. The invention of the printing press was of great importance and enjoyed immediate success throughout Europe. Printing centers were quickly established throughout the continent. Both Milan and Venice were among the most important of these printing centers.

The *Parrot Room* in the Davanzati Palace in Florence. The frescoes are typical of the style of interior decorating popular near the end of the fourteenth century. The clothing worn by the two women in the picture shows the refined style of Italian fashion at that time.

THE NEW WORLD

New Ships

As the population began to increase again in Western Europe, so did the demand for food. Local supplies of food were no longer able to keep up with demand. Heavy agricultural products such as grain, salt, and wine had to be shipped over long distances. Port cities were able to receive these supplies by sea. Genoa, for example, imported food not only from Mediterranean countries, but also from lands bordering the Black Sea and the North Sea. At the end of the *Reconquista* period, the Straits of Gibraltar were once more opened to shipping, and the Mediterranean Sea was united with the Atlantic Ocean and the North Sea.

Ships now had to sail for long distances far from the coast. The cost of transporting goods by ship was high and would remain so unless newer, bigger ships capable of traveling long distances with large loads were built. The ships of the day, called galleys, became taller and wider, and capable of carrying two hundred or three hundred tons of cargo. But, for the most part, these ships were still too fragile and fell easy prey to pirates. For this reason, Venice began to organize and protect convoys of at least six galleys.

In the fifteenth century, the Venetians and Genoese designed even more sophisticated ships larger than previous vessels. These new ships were two or three decks deep and had a quarterdeck and a foredeck. The ships, called galleons, were built with three masts and carried a huge number of sails.

These new ships were able to transport up to one thousand tons of goods, and were designed to better weather storms. They were able to stay at sea longer and could sail from Spain to Flanders or England without stopping. It was on these new ships that Italian and Spanish sailors, and then sailors from other nations, learned the skills needed to sail the high seas. These skills were essential for those who later took long voyages to unknown lands.

Christopher Columbus

It is now known that as early as the tenth century, Viking explorers reached the coast of North America. The Vikings did not establish regular contact with the area, and America remained an unknown land to Europeans.

During the late fifteenth century, the desire to find an all-water route to the riches of India and China led to the geographic discoveries made at the time. Demonstrating an extraordinary mix of determination and courage, the Italian navigator Christopher Columbus man-

aged to get the support of Queen Isabella of Spain and sailed west from Spain in August 1492. In October he reached a small island that he called San Salvador. Until his death, Columbus was convinced he had reached the East Indies and not stumbled upon a new land.

The First Results of the New Discoveries

In 1494 Portugal and Spain signed the Treaty of Tordesillas, which established a line of longitude 100 leagues (about 340 miles) west of the Azores as the dividing line between Spanish and Portuguese spheres of influence. Spain was granted control of new discoveries and trade west of the line, and Portugal was granted similar control east of the line.

In 1499 Amerigo Vespucci set sail on a trip to explore the mouth of the Amazon River. Vespucci made maps of his discoveries and signed his name on these maps. His name, Amerigo, became identified with the new lands, which came to be called America.

In 1500 Pedro Cabral, a Portuguese explorer landed on what is now the eastern tip of Brazil. Since this part of the South American continent is east of the line of demarcation, Portugal claimed and later colonized Brazil.

The Spanish continued exploring their new world. Cuba had been reached by Columbus in 1492, and a Spanish colony was started in 1511. In 1513 the explorer Vasco Núñez de Balboa crossed the Isthmus of Panama to find another vast ocean. At first sight, this body of water seemed to be peaceful, which is how the Pacific Ocean got its name.

In April 1519, Hernán Cortés, a Spanish soldier and adventurer, landed in Mexico at a place he called Veracruz. Under the leadership of Cortés, the Spanish conquered the Aztecs. In September of the same year, Ferdinand Magellan left Spain with five ships on a journey that would eventually develop into the first voyage around the world.

One of the important consequences of the discovery of the new lands was the development of the slave trade. At first Native Americans were used to work the mines and plantations in the colonies, as shown in the pictures on the left side of the map. Soon, however, the Portuguese began to import slaves from Africa. The picture on the right side of the map shows African slaves being loaded onto ships.
The slaves were usually captured by other Africans and then sold to the Portuguese. The slaves were chained and crowded into ships. Many died on the voyage to the Americas. Those who survived faced lives of unrelenting work.
The riches from the Americas were shipped to ports in Europe. The products of the New World poured especially into the Spanish port of Seville, which is shown in the picture in the center of the page.

(The background map on these pages was copied from a navigational chart now found in the Estense Library in Modena, Italy.)

CHARLES V

A Grand Inheritance

At the height of his power, Charles V, Holy Roman emperor, king of Germany, king of Spain, and king of Naples, ruled over an empire upon which "the sun never set." His empire even included all of the Spanish lands in the Americas. Charles was a member of the Hapsburg family, but he was also related to the houses of Aragon, Castile, and Burgundy.

The future Charles V was born in Ghent in 1500 and grew up in Mechlin (in present-day Belgium). His teachers were Spanish and Flemish, and from the latter he absorbed the severe spirit of the new religious devotion. Between 1515 and 1519, Charles inherited all the territories of the four noble houses from which he was descended. By the time he was twenty, Charles ruled over Austria, part of southern Germany, Spain and its possessions in the Americas, Naples, Sicily, Sardinia, Franche-Comte, and the Low Countries.

When the Holy Roman Emperor Maximilian I died in 1519, Charles was elected emperor, defeating the French king, Francis I. The power of the Hapsburg family reached its peak in 1526, when Charles' brother, Ferdinand, became king of Bohemia and Hungary. With this final move, the Hapsburg Empire came face to face with the Ottoman Turks in southeastern Europe.

A Complex Empire

Having such a large empire meant that Charles V had to deal with many perplexing problems. Each part of his empire presented different types of problems, which Charles attacked with great energy and the help of talented and intelligent advisors.

The first major difficulties appeared in Spain. Charles was regarded as a foreigner in Spain because he had been raised in Flanders and used Flemish officials to administer his rule in Spain. Some of the cities in Spain revolted when new taxes were levied. With the help of the Spanish nobles, Charles repressed the revolt in 1521.

A revolt in Germany also took place at the same time as the Spanish revolt. A league of knights, the Knights of the Rhine, was formed in Germany with the aim of seizing lands and riches that belonged to the Roman Catholic church. This took place in the early years of the Reformation (see page 57), when Protestants began resisting the power of the church. The league failed in its aims, and the revolt was crushed.

Troubles With France

When Charles V became emperor, France found itself surrounded by Hapsburg territories. King Francis I of France, an ambitious man left with little room to expand his territory, moved south into Italy. In 1515 the French conquered the duchy of Milan. Francis made no secret of the fact that he had his eyes set on expanding into southern Italy, which was then ruled by the Hapsburgs. When the French tried to move farther south, they were defeated by Charles' troops at Pavia in 1525.

The French then joined with the English, Florentines, Venetians, Milanese, and Papal States to form the League of Cognac to fight the empire in Italy. The league's challenge to the empire failed. In 1529 the Peace Treaty of Cambrai was signed and Francis I gave up his ambitions regarding Italy.

The Last Medieval Ruler

In 1555 Charles V, sick and exhausted by political events, renounced his sovereignty over the Low Countries and all his other hereditary titles in favor of his son, Philip II of Spain. Charles then retired to a monastery where he died in 1558.

In his lifetime Charles had been guided by the ideal of creating a Christian empire that could lead the Western world. But such a plan was out of the question in fifteenth century Europe. There was no unity in the Christian world after the Protestant Reformation began, and Charles' rule over his lands was not absolute. In practice, it proved impossible to organize a centralized government for such a large and varied empire. Castile exercised power over Spain, while the House of Aragon played a similar role in the Italian dominions. What really happened was the Hapsburg possessions outside of Germany came under Spanish influence, and the Flemish part of the empire lost its importance. This loss of influence in the western part of the empire was not offset by any increase in authority in Germany where the princes and cities, both Roman Catholic and Protestant, had no intention of giving up their independence.

A more modern Europe was developing. It was a Europe composed of nations in which each sovereign became more powerful within his or her own country and was not part of a greater empire. Charles did not create a strong centralized government, and for this reason he can be considered the last medieval ruler.

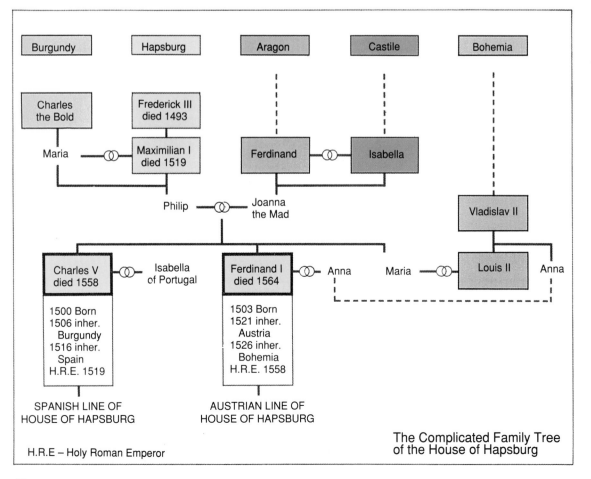

The Complicated Family Tree of the House of Hapsburg

A cameo portrait of Charles V. *(Vienna, Museum of Art History)*

Ghent, the native city of Charles V. This illustration was inspired by a painting by Jan van Eyck. (*The Mystic Angel* in St. Bovone's Church, Ghent).

The Hapsburg Coat of Arms.

THE TURKS: A NEW EUROPEAN POWER

Ottoman Power at its Height

The power of the Ottoman Empire reached its height in the early years of the sixteenth century. Under Süleyman the Magnificent (1494–1566), the Ottomans ruled lands in North Africa, eastern Asia, and southeastern Europe. They also controlled all the lands around the Black Sea, turning that body of water into a Turkish lake. It was during this time that the Ottomans became a powerful threat to the Hapsburgs. In 1526 the Ottomans conquered most of Hungary, but their surge into eastern Europe was stopped at the Battle of Vienna in 1529.

The Ottoman government was embodied in the sultan, who had absolute power. He appointed a grand vizier, the governors of each province, and the heads of the army. The grand vizier's role was to supervise the administration of the government. The role of the army was to conquer new territories and defend the empire as a whole. From a political point of view, the Ottoman Empire appeared unassailable, and Europe looked elsewhere to satisfy its desire for political and economic expansion.

Life Within the Empire

The inhabitants of the empire were divided into Muslims and non-Muslims. For the most part, the non-Muslim group was composed of Jews and Christians. Muslims did not have to pay taxes; non-Muslims paid taxes for the protection they received from the sultan.

The Ottoman reputation for religious tolerance was well-known throughout the Mediterranean world. When the Jews were driven out of Spain by the Inquisition in the sixteenth century, many took refuge in Constantinople and Morocco.

The Ottomans opened their arms to cultural influences from the rest of the world. Süleyman the Magnificent was a cultured man, and the first Ottoman chronicles were drawn together during his reign. Scientific study was also encouraged. This period is remembered for its architectural splendor, as Constantinople again became a magnificent city, admired by travelers from all over the world.

The Commercial Agreement

In 1535 Süleyman the Magnificent granted the French king, Francis I, special commercial privileges. France offered no threat to the Ottoman Empire at the time, and, by striking a deal with the Turks, Francis I hoped to reduce Hapsburg pressure on France.

The most important result of this agreement was the permanent installation of French consuls in several cities throughout the Ottoman Empire. The consuls played the part of mediators between the Ottoman government and the French citizens who lived under its authority. Nomination of the consuls was usually in the hands of French merchants who conducted business in the Ottoman Empire and lived there. Little by little, French merchants, followed by the Dutch and the English, settled in Ottoman ports and in major inland cities, forming alliances with the non-Turkish populations. In the long run, these merchants and consuls acquired the ability to play a direct role in the internal affairs of the empire.

An Ottoman ceramic vase dating about 1500. Minor arts such as the making and decorating of everyday objects, were practiced to a high degree of expertise in the Ottoman Empire. Artisans, belonging to craft associations, were subject to rigid rules that insured the production of high quality objects.

This portrait of Francis I was painted by Jean Clouet and can be found in the Louvre Museum in Paris. Francis governed France from 1515 to 1547. He established and maintained close ties with the Ottoman sultans, hoping these alliances would reduce Hapsburg pressure against France.

In this scene Turkish forces prepare for the Battle of Mohacs in Hungary in 1526. The Turks won the battle and went on to conquer Hungary.

Istanbul

Baghdad

Cairo

This map shows the progressive expansion of the Ottoman Empire. The Turkish advance seemed impossible to halt. The northern coasts of Africa, western Asia, and eastern Europe became parts of the empire. The Hapsburgs were able to stop the Turkish advance in Europe, but links between the Ottomans and France allowed the Ottomans to become a leading factor in international European politics.

THE MAJOR FEATURES OF THE MODERN NATION

Politically, the history of the fourteenth and fifteenth centuries in Europe can be viewed as one long struggle to centralize the power of government. Throughout most of the Middle Ages, the nations we know today as France, Germany, Spain, and Italy were actually little more than geographic areas. They were composed of many smaller territories ruled over by a collection of princes, dukes, barons, and other assorted nobles. Cities within these areas sometimes ruled themselves, or were ruled by powerful families or princes, and the Roman Catholic church not only played a religious role in the life of the state, but a political role as well.

All these forces, independent cities, the church, and the nobility usually tried to maintain their power and fought against centralizing power in the hands of a national leader. But, by the end of the fifteenth century, some countries in Europe, notably France, Spain, and England did begin to centralize political power in the hands of a king or queen, and the foundations of the modern political state, or nation, were set in place. The strength of this new type of state lay in the monarch's control over the government, the courts, the treasury, tax collection, the army, and most of the other important functions and responsibilities of a modern country.

The Concentration of Royal Power

As modern states developed, political power tended to become identified and concentrated in the monarchy itself. This was probably due, in part, to the strong personalities of certain kings such as Louis XI and Francis I in France, and Henry VIII in England. This concentration of power meant the king no longer had to consult with his nobles before he decreed a law. Still, the monarch was subject to pressure from the people, nobles and commoners alike, who made up the royal court. These people were called courtiers, and they usually wanted something from the king.

Sometimes the royal courts grew to enormous sizes. The court of Francis I numbered at least one thousand people. These large courts often split into different factions, which competed for the favors of the monarch, making it difficult for him or her to deal quickly with so many different requests. It was for this reason that a fundamental organ of modern government began to develop at this time. This organ was the king's council or secret council.

As modern nations developed, kings gathered around themselves advisers who helped them govern. This illustration shows nobles from the court of Francis I in France attending to administrative matters concerning the government of the nation.

The king's council was made up of a small group of advisers, perhaps a dozen, who were close to the king and who helped him make decisions in the quickest and most effective way possible. The council members were usually experts in the different functions of government —taxation, finance, law, and military affairs. These councilors, or secretaries of state, usually came from the monarch's family, the army, the church, and the aristocracy.

On occasion one member of the council would have more power than all the other members, and kings or queens sometimes had favorites. Such personalities had existed in the past. As modern states developed, however, and more power was concentrated in the monarch, the presence of these people became a major element in the government of a kingdom. These people became an essential and accepted part of the team that, together with the monarch, led the country.

The administration of justice in the Western European nations tended to follow the lines set down by Roman law, but with one major difference. The king himself was the sole source of justice, and no one disobeyed him. The king alone chose those people who would administer his justice. This development happened rather quickly in England, took longer in France, and was a total failure in Germany, where the local princes continued to administer justice, and the emperor had no way to stop them. As a result, government in Germany remained fragmented.

Toward Absolute Monarchy

The monarch was constantly surrounded by courtiers, admirers, and flatterers, whose major fear was that of losing grace before their sovereign. As the printing press became more common, these courtiers would write and distribute pamphlets flattering the king, who became almost an object of religious devotion.

The idea that the king should consult his subjects before making decisions had never totally disappeared, especially when he had to convince them to pay more taxes. England did have a parliament composed of a House of Lords and a House of Commons, but as the English kings grew more powerful, Parliament merely approved the monarch's decisions.

In France, King Francis I governed through the use of decrees without consulting the nobility, and the nobility did not protest too loudly. Francis seemed to know how to respond to his subjects' needs. This meant that Francis identified himself with the nation and that his subjects recognized him as a single leader who, in theory, took care of the entire realm.

Cardinal Bibbiena receiving the homage of a visitor in his Vatican apartments decorated with frescoes painted by Raphael.

ROME ON THE EVE OF THE REFORMATION

The Reformation was a religious movement that began in the first half of the sixteenth century and saw the establishment of Protestantism. The corruption of the Roman Catholic church during the late fifteenth and early sixteenth centuries is often cited as the cause of the Reformation. Without question some of the actions of some church leaders at this time, especially the Borgia popes, were morally objectionable. However, it would be oversimplifying the matter to cite papal corruption as the major or only cause of the Reformation.

Dissatisfaction with the church and how it operated was nothing new. For centuries there had been conflicts between the church and various political leaders in Europe, sometimes breaking out into open warfare. There had also been, over the centuries, protests against certain teachings of the church. John Wycliffe and Jan Hus were only two of these protesters.

The Reformation, however, was something bigger and different. It was based not only on religious differences, but also cultural and political causes.

Cultural Causes

Humanism and the Renaissance had produced new ideas not only about religion but also about the very nature of human life and its relationship to the world around it. By learning Greek, scholars had been able to go back to some of the earliest versions of Holy Scripture and found that what was written there was not always the same as what was found in the Latin scriptures then available.

Even when humanists chose to remain in the church, they began to evolve a different faith, one that was more spiritual and had little room for rites and ceremonies. This fresh approach to Christianity was not limited to a few, isolated intellectuals. The principles of the modern devotions were practiced by many common people in their daily worship, and even at home. This movement was especially widespread in Germany and in the Low Countries in the fifteenth century.

The invention of the printing press meant more books were being printed and circulated. More people learned how to read, and those who already knew how to read had more access to both established and new ideas.

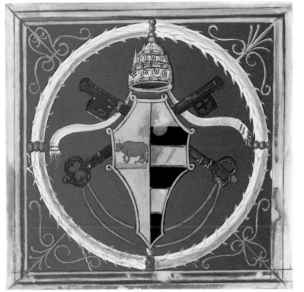

Political Causes

As modern political nations developed in the fifteenth century, antagonisms between the new, stronger political leaders and the church grew. This type of dispute was not new. For centuries popes and monarchs, bishops and dukes, and religious and political leaders on all levels had fought over political and religious power. What was new was the intensity and degree of the current struggles. The sovereigns and princes regarded the church as a political power, and it was.

In 1478 King Louis XI of France stopped the church from persecuting members of a religious group known as Waldenses in the Dauphine region of France. The king was not particularly interested in saving the Waldenses from bloody persecution, but the Dauphine was French, and the king maintained that no one else was allowed to persecute France's citizens. By the early fifteenth century, the popes could no longer rely on the intervention of a prince or king in times of need.

Attempts at Reform

The need for reform had come, and the church made several attempts at reforming itself from within. New monastic orders of friars were created, like the Order of St. Francis of Paola in southern Italy. These friars led simple lives, and the secular clergy was encouraged to help the new orders in their efforts to reach the faithful.

In 1512 Pope Julius II called the Fifth Lateran Council together to discuss many of the problems facing the church. The council worked out an agreement between France and the church, solving some of the disagreements between the two powers. The Fifth Lateran Council remained in session until 1517, the year Martin Luther openly challenged the authority of the church and began the Reformation.

Portrait of Philip Melanchthon, the author of *Augsburg Confession*, a document written in 1530 that presents basic Lutheran principles.

Portrait of Martin Luther.

This illustration shows a scene from the Peasants' War in Germany. The poor felt that Lutheran doctrine would liberate them from the miserable conditions in which they lived.

THE PROTESTANT REFORMATION

Martin Luther

Martin Luther was born in Saxony, in 1483. He first studied law but later entered an Augustine monastery and studied for the priesthood. After being ordained a priest in 1507, Luther taught theology at the University of Wittenberg in Saxony. During a trip to Rome in 1511, he was shocked by what he considered a lack of morality there.

When he returned to Wittenberg, he studied and lectured on the writings of St. Paul. He received his Doctor of Theology degree in 1512 and became a professor of theology. He became convinced that salvation depended on faith alone. The church, however, taught that salvation depended on a combination of grace and good works. Between 1512 and 1517, Luther's ideas remained within the confines of the university at Wittenberg, but then he became embroiled in controversy.

The Ninety-Five Theses

The immediate cause of the controversy was Luther's denunciation of the church's teachings about indulgences. An indulgence was a full or partial remission of the punishment a person would face after death for sins that had been committed. Indulgences could be won by doing good works, or they could be purchased. Bankers, bishops, and important merchants made every effort to obtain lucrative contracts from the church to collect the money paid by the faithful for indulgences.

Luther believed selling indulgences was wrong. He was especially incensed by the selling of indulgences near Wittenberg by Johann Tetzel, a Dominican friar. Luther denied the theory that indulgences were a means of obtaining salvation. He summarized his ideas on indulgences and other religious matters in Ninety-five Theses, which he posted on the door of the castle church in Wittenberg in 1517.

The theses were publicly discussed and created a great deal of excitement. Because of the controversy he stirred up, Luther was summoned to Rome to defend his ideas, but he did not go. At this point, it might still have been possible for the pope and Luther to reach some form of agreement, for Luther had not yet proclaimed his more radical ideas. Finally, in 1519 Luther openly broke all ties with Rome and challenged the pope's powers.

Luther held there was no difference between the faithful and the clergy and that every individual had the right to read the sacred texts without being required to follow the church's interpretation. He then translated the Bible into German.

Luther also taught that salvation was possible through faith alone and that the only sacraments that were truly valid were baptism and Holy Communion. These were the fundamental points of Luther's position and, in response, Pope Leo X excommunicated Luther from the Roman Catholic church.

From the Peasants' War to the Peace of Augsburg

Luther received massive support in Germany. Many princes accepted his doctrines as a way of affirming their own autonomy and increasing their independence from the emperor, who had traditionally been the defender of Christianity.

Along with support from the princes, Luther's ideas also received support from the peasants. Many poor people interpreted Luther's declaration of religious independence as a confirmation of a wider form of freedom, a freedom that would put an end to the abuses they had suffered at the hands of their rulers. This feeling was partially responsible for a peasants' revolt in 1524 led by Thomas Münzer, another leader of the Reformation. Luther did not approve of this revolt and he urged those in power to repress it.

Luther's appeal was openly welcomed by the authorities. The revolt was crushed, and Münzer was captured and killed. Germany, however remained a battleground between Protestants and Roman Catholics, and between those princes and cities that supported the Reformation and those forces that remained loyal to the emperor. Civil war seemed inevitable, until both sides reached a compromise in the Treaty of Augsburg in 1555.

Under the terms of the treaty, princes were granted the right to follow Lutheran doctrine if they wanted to, but the common people were obliged to follow the religion of their rulers, be it Roman Catholic or Protestant. Any church possessions seized by Protestant princes before 1555 remained their property.

One result of the treaty was that, since the choice of Lutheranism depended on the power of the princes, the religion actually spread less and less. The task of spreading Protestantism then passed to John Calvin.

Frontispiece of Luther's German translation of the Bible.

THE SPREAD OF PROTESTANTISM

Portrait of Zwingli, who first brought Protestantism to Switzerland.

New Developments

Luther's teachings spread far beyond Germany, and the Reformation as a whole was inextricably woven into the pattern of political, social, and cultural changes taking place in Europe in the sixteenth century. Lutheranism was welcomed and supported by the Swedish and Danish monarchs, and they helped it spread into Finland and Norway. As the reform movement grew, it also splintered into many different branches.

The Reformation leader in Switzerland was Ulrich Zwingli, a humanist who had studied the works of Erasmus. Zwingli reorganized local churches along Protestant lines in the Swiss cities of Zurich, Berne, and Basel. His attitude toward the sacrament of Holy Communion differed from Luther's. For Zwingli, Holy Communion, or the Lord's Supper, was purely symbolic in nature, while Luther felt the sacrament was a source of God's grace. Zwingli's views received wide support in Switzerland, but they separated him from Lutheran doctrine and cost him the military support of the German Protestants. In Switzerland, as in other parts of Europe, the split between Roman Catholics and Protestants developed into violence, and Zwingli was killed in 1531 in a war between supporters of the two religions.

John Calvin

John Calvin was born and educated in France, which remained a Roman Catholic country throughout the Reformation. Forced to flee France in 1534, Calvin took refuge in Switzerland where he became an important Protestant thinker and leader.

While living in the Swiss city of Basel, Calvin wrote his fundamental work, *Institutes of the Christian Religion*. Calvin reiterated many of the principles of the earlier reformers, citing the Bible as the source of Christian belief, rejecting the authority of the pope, and reaffirming the superiority of faith over good works.

Calvin also taught that salvation was the free gift of God; that there was no way anyone could know who God chose to save. Those chosen to be saved by God were called the Elect. People's duty, according to Calvin, was to live their lives according to the Sacred Scriptures in order to glorify God. Only those who lived this way could hope to be among the Elect.

Calvin moved from Basel to Geneva where he became the leader of the Protestant pastors in the city. The strict policies of Calvin and the Protestant pastors alienated the political leadership in Geneva, and Calvin was forced to leave the city for a time. He was welcomed back later, and in 1541 established a church based on his doctrines.

Pastors in Calvinist churches were leaders of the religious community. The doctors of the church were responsible for teaching doctrine, and the older members of the church, or presbyters, were expected to give moral leadership and guidance to church members. The pastors and presbyters together formed the consistory, which exercised control over the whole community.

The success of such rigidly organized religion depended upon the strong faith of its believers and often on the support of the local political authorities. The new doctrine touched every aspect of life thereby reducing the division between religious and everyday existence. For Calvinists, even the most humble activity was a task God had given an individual to do. It was the duty of the believers to carry out these tasks to the best of their ability.

Calvinism spread throughout Europe except for Germany and Scandinavia. Calvinist believers in France were called Huguenots, and the conflict between Roman Catholics and Huguenots led to open warfare in the latter part of the sixteenth century. Calvinism also spread to Scotland where the preacher John Knox converted large numbers of the aristocracy and established the Church of Scotland.

The Church of England

The separation of England from the Roman Catholic Church was the direct result of the refusal of Pope Clement VII to annul the marriage of King Henry VIII to his first wife, Catherine of Aragon. The marriage had produced no male heirs for the crown of England.

When the pope refused to grant the annulment, Henry declared that the Pope had no authority over the church in England. He divorced his wife and married Anne Boleyn, a young woman of the royal court. Henry then persuaded the English Parliament to support his actions. Parliament passed two acts, one freeing the English church from papal rule and one declaring Henry as head of the Church of England.

The king then proceeded to seize all church property in England and to close the Roman Catholic monasteries and convents. Henry accepted some aspects of Lutheranism, but, for the most part, he was concerned with establishing control of the church within the monarchy and silencing all opposition.

This illustration shows Calvin in Basel, Switzerland, where he wrote his fundamental work, *Institutes of the Christian Religion*.

Portrait of Henry VIII of England. His separation from the Roman Catholic church was more a political than a religious action.

REFORM WITHIN THE CATHOLIC CHURCH

The desire to reform the Roman Catholic church had existed long before the advent of Martin Luther and the Reformation. Religious and political leaders throughout Europe were well aware of the problems within the church, as were ordinary believers. However, none of the popes, including those who were humanist scholars, were able to exercise the type of leadership capable of responding to the need for basic reform. They were also unable to deal with religious leaders like Martin Luther or political leaders like Charles V.

During the fifteenth century some efforts at reform had been made. In 1458 Pope Pius II invited the great thinker Cardinal Nicolo Cusano to Rome to reform the clergy within the diocese of Rome itself. Throughout the century new monastic orders were created to work with the poor.

The Society of Jesus

The Society of Jesus was a new religious order founded in response to the Reformation. It became very powerful and influential. The Society was established by Ignatius Loyola, a Spanish noble and soldier who gave up his riches and his military career to follow a religious life.

The Society was officially recognized by the church in 1540. Its members, called Jesuits, not only took the traditional vows, but also took an additional vow of obedience to the pope. It took many years of study and devotion to become a Jesuit priest. The Jesuits established missions in all parts of the world and took a great interest in the education of the young. They also played a leading role in the reformation of the Roman Catholic church from within.

The Council of Trent

The Council of Trent was called in reaction to the Reformation and to institute reforms in the Roman Catholic church. The council met for the first time in December 1545 in the Cathedral of Trent in northern Italy. The religious leaders who formed the council had to deal with two major problems. First, the council had to define the position of the Roman Catholic church in response to Protestant criticism. Second, the council had to identify those areas of reform necessary for a complete renewal of the church as a whole.

The Frontispiece of the *Index of Prohibited Books*, a list of books banned by the church in the sixteenth century. The Index is no longer in effect.

The Council of Trent in session.

During the first period of the council, which lasted four years, a list of sacred books was drawn up. The council identified these books as sources of inspiration and essential to the church's existence. The council also drew up a list of forbidden books commonly called the *Index*.

The council went on to confirm the church's belief in the theory of Original Sin and defined Roman Catholic doctrine regarding the seven sacraments. The council recognized the importance of Christian tradition in establishing basic beliefs. Decrees were issued by the council regarding the study of Sacred Scriptures and the duties of bishops.

The council adjourned in 1547 and scheduled its next meeting for 1549 but actually resumed sessions in 1551. French representatives of the church did not attend the second session which spent a full year debating the nature of the sacraments, especially penance and Holy Communion. The council was suspended again in 1552 when war broke out in Germany. It did not meet again until 1562.

During its last session, the council prepared its final position on the sacraments and formulated its decrees on reform. Council decrees outlined how parish priests should be trained and listed the requirements for pastoral guidance within the local areas of the church. The need for the clergy to preach and instruct was emphasized, and a definition of religious life was given.

At the end of 1564, Pope Pius IV ratified and published all the decrees issued by the council. He then formed a commission of eight cardinals to oversee the interpretation and execution of the decrees.

Ignatius Loyola, the founder of the Society of Jesus.

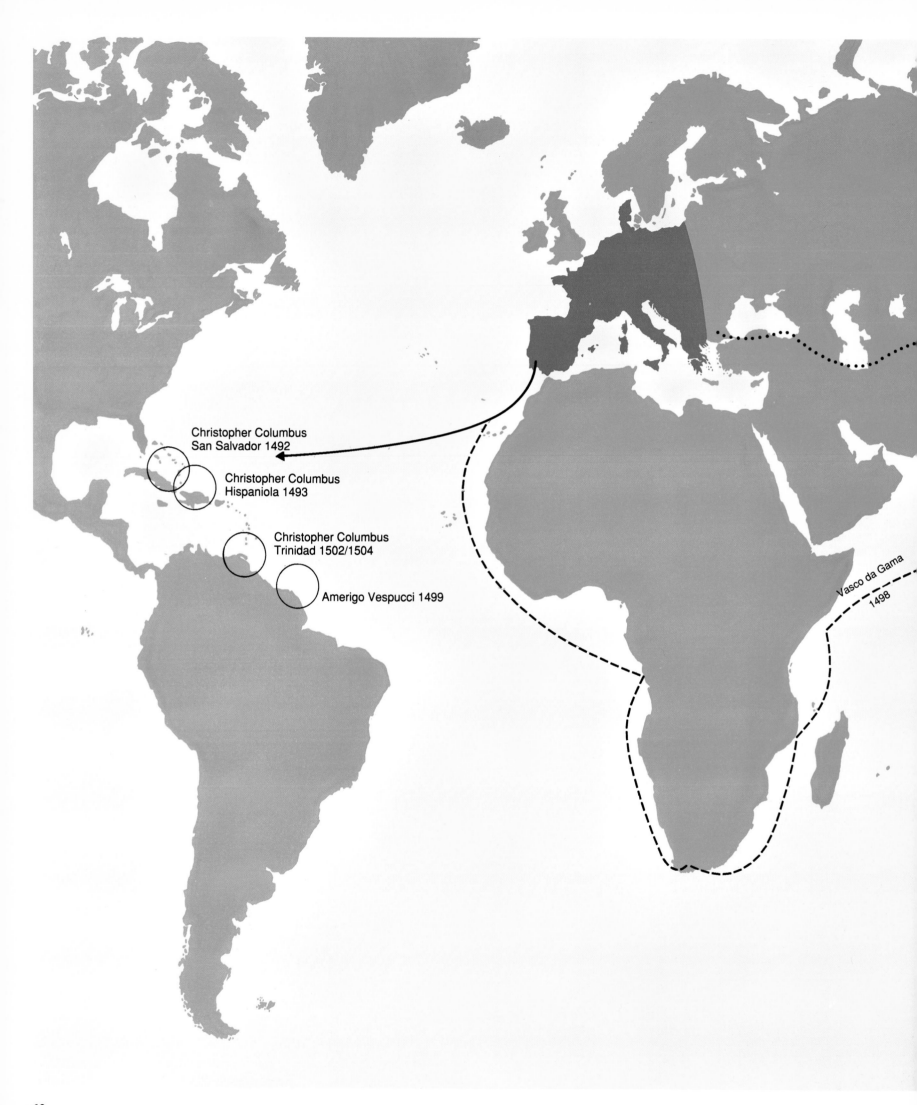

Christopher Columbus
San Salvador 1492

Christopher Columbus
Hispaniola 1493

Christopher Columbus
Trinidad 1502/1504

Amerigo Vespucci 1499

Vasco da Gama
1498

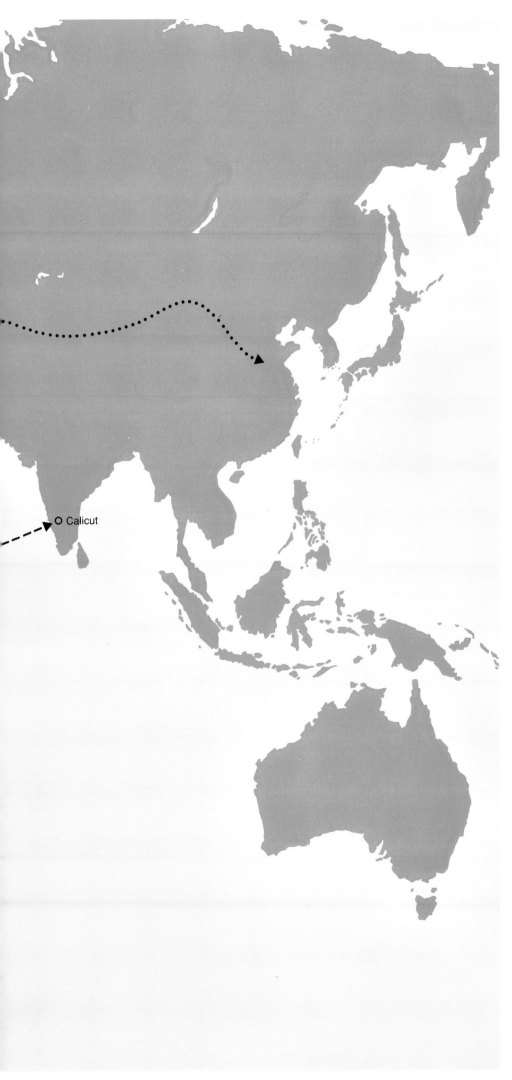

VOYAGES OF DISCOVERY ON LAND AND SEA

Goods and travelers from Europe had always been well received in the Far East. During the thirteenth and fourteenth centuries, the Mongolian Empire had looked with favor on the intrepid caravans of Europeans which carefully avoided the Islamic world. However, the rise of the Turkish Empire forced European merchants to find better and faster ways to the Far East. Europeans began looking for a way to India around Africa. The Europeans also believed that they could reach China by sailing west from Europe. This search for new routes eventually led to the Americas and a new episode in history.

O Calicut

KEY

◄• • • • • • • • • • The overland route to the Far East followed by the silk merchants and fourteenth century missionaries from Europe.

◄ – – – – – – The passage to the east around Africa.

◄———————— The passage to the east across the Atlantic Ocean.

GLOSSARY

act: law made by a legislative body such as an Act of Congress or Parliament

almshouse: house founded by charity in which poor people, no longer able to earn money, may live without paying rent

appanage: property belonging to somebody because of inheritance or by right of political office

artisan: a worker skilled in industry or trade

basilica: an early Christian church having an oblong plan, a high central area separated by columns from aisles at each side, and an apse (recess) at the east end

bull: an official order or announcement from the Pope

commune: small territorial district for purposes of governmental administration

concistory: (or presbyter) court of priests, clergymen, or presbyters to deal with church business

contemporary: belonging to the same time, living at the same time

crusade: military expedition made by Christian rulers and people of Europe during the Middle Ages to recover the Holy Land from the Muslims

decree: order given by a ruler or authority and having the force of a law

doctrine: what is taught as true by a church

dominion: territory of a sovereign government

duchy: land ruled by a duke or duchess

dynasty: succession of rulers belonging to one family

ecumenical: of or representing the whole Christian world, or universal church; seeking to restore the unity of the Christian churches

enclosure: an area of land that is surrounded by a barrier

fiscal: of public revenue

galleon: Spanish sailing ship (fifteenth-seventeenth centuries) with a high stern

guild: society of persons organized to help one another, with such common interests as trade or social welfare

heir: person with a legal right to receive a title or property when the owner dies

heresy: a religious belief rejected by church authorities as contrary to the established beliefs of the church

heretic: a person who believes in a heresy

***hermandad*:** Spanish league of cities in the fifteenth and sixteenth centuries

***hidalgos*:** Spanish nobles at the time of the Renaissance

intermediary: somebody or something acting as a link between persons or groups

Islam: faith or religion, proclaimed by the prophet Muhammad; all Muslims, all the Muslim world

Khan: title used by some rulers and officials in Afghanistan, Central Asia, in olden times title used by supreme rulers of Turkish, Tatar, and Mongol tribes

Khanate: territory ruled over by a Khan

layperson: a person who is not a priest or member of a religious order

lithograph: something, especially a picture, printed from parts of a flat stone or sheet of zinc or aluminum that are prepared to receive a greasy ink

manuscript: book as first written out by hand, or typed

marquisate: land owned by a marquis or marquess

mausoleum: a large, usually stone, tomb built above ground

mercantile: of, or relating, to trade, commerce, and merchants

Muslim: one who professes Islam; follower of Muhammad

nomad: a member of a group that moves from place to place, usually to find pasture for the group's herd of animals

oligarchy: government by a small group of all-powerful persons

orthodox: a belief or practice that conforms to established doctrine, especially church doctrine

papacy: the position, rank, or authority of the pope; the term of the pope's rule

papal: of, having to do with, or belonging to the pope

patriarch: a bishop or leader in the Eastern Orthodox church

plague: a disease that is highly contagious, widespread, and often fatal

pope: supreme head of the Roman Catholic church

presbyter: a church elder

principality: country ruled by a prince

pustule: pimple or blister, especially one filled with pus

ransom: freeing of a captive on payment; sum of money paid for a captive's release

ratify: to confirm an agreement by signature or other formality

reformation: radical change for the better in social, political, or religious affairs

renaissance: a new birth; revival

republic: a country with a system of government in which the elected representatives of the people are supreme, with a non-hereditary head, and non-hereditary privileged class or classes

sack: the violent plunder by a victorious army of a captured city or area

schism: offense of causing the division of an organization, especially a church, into two or more groups, usually through a difference of opinion

seigniory: territory ruled by a lord, especially in Renaissance Italy

sovereignty: ability of a state to be fully self-governing and independent in foreign affairs

sultan: Muslim ruler, especially of the former Ottoman Empire

temporal: of earthly human life; not spiritual

Teutonic: of the Germanic peoples (including Scandinavian and Anglo-Saxon peoples)

tillage: process of cultivating the land

xylographics: the art of printing on wood by means of a woodcut

INDEX

N

Naples 18-20, 28, 48
Navarre 11
New World 42, 46-47
Normandy 10, 12-13, 39
North Sea 33, 42, 46
Nuremberg 34

O

Oder River 33
Order of St. Francis of Paola 55
Order of the Golden Fleece 40
Orthodox Church 7
Osman 9
Ottoman Chronicles 50
Ottoman Dynasty 9
Ottoman Empire 6, 9, 50-51
Oxford University 26

P

Pacific Ocean 47
Padua 20
Palmieri, Matteo 19
Papal States 19, 29, 48
Paris 12-13, 16, 39, 44, 50
Peasants' Revolt 57
Peasants' War 56-57
Perugia 20
Peruzzi 24
Petrarch 18, 22
Philip I (Hapsburg) 40
Philip IV, king of France (the Fair) 10
Philip VI of Valois 10
Philip the Bold, duke of Burgundy 11

Philip the Good 40
Pisa 20, 28
Pius II, pope 60
Pius IV, pope 61
plagues 14-15, 16, 17, 34
Plantagenets 10
Poland 37
population 7, 9, 14-15, 17, 46
Portugal 4, 24, 42, 47
Pragmatic Sanction 29
Prague, University of 27
Protestant Reformation 4, 48, 57
Protestantism 54, 57, 59

R

Reconquista period 46
Reformation 4, 44, 48, 54-55, 57, 59-60
Reims 12
Renaissance 4, 44, 54
revolts 11-12, 16-17, 34
Rhine River 33, 40-41
Richard III, king of England 38
Rienzo, Cola di 19
Riga 36
Roman Catholic church 6, 9, 26, 29, 34, 44, 48, 52, 54, 57, 59-60
Roman Catholic Reformation 60-61
Roman Empire 4, 6-7, 16, 20, 22, 26, 33, 41-42
Roman law 53
Romanians 7
Rome 6, 19, 22, 28, 44, 54-55, 57, 60
Rouen 12
Russia 8-9

S

T

U

V